New Edda

To order additional copies, please contact us.
BookSurge, LLC
www.booksurge.com
1-866-308-6235
orders@booksurge.com

New Edda

Wayland Skallagrimsson

2003

New Edda

There are many to whom I would dedicate this book. I wish to dedicate it to my family, and especially my parents, who brought me up to make up my own damn mind about religion. I would like to dedicate it to my ancestors. I would like to dedicate it to Steve, my blood brother. I would like to dedicate it to John Cyr, my kinsman from Maine, and to his wife Carrie, and to their children. I would like to dedicate this book to Paulo Munhoz of Brazil, my good friend and a tru man who is bringing the old faith to life in a new land. I would like to dedicate it to the Raven Kindred North, in thanks for their hospitality, generosity, and friendship. I would like to dedicate it to Jarl Hakon, without whom our religion would not now be alive. I would like to dedicate it to the gods and goddesses, the alfs and idises, the ancestors and heroes. Most especially would I like to dedicate this book to my patron Odin, without whom it would not have been written. I would dedicate it to Loki, who has played such a big part in my life. I would dedicate it to my disir, my personal goddesses: Bondweaver, Axana, Wynn, Rachel. And last but most certainly not least I would dedicate it to my Lady, my Door, my Oenochoe.

Introduction

Asatru is the modern name given by some to the worship of the gods of the Norse people, who are popularly and somewhat inaccurately known as vikings. It literally means "true to the Aesir". The earliest written records we have of these people date to the height of the Roman Empire, with such travelogue writers as Tacitus. He described tribes of what he called the Germani, which is simply a Latin word that means "foreigner", or "barbarian". They lived on the borders of the Roman Empire, which sometimes was an enemy to them and sometimes an employer, for many Germani made much of their money from hiring themselves out as mercenaries. Tacitus describes religious beliefs that seem consistent with the later Norse mythology as recorded by Snorri and Saemundr (or whoever it was actually collected together the Poetic Edda). He describes tribes that, by modern standards, lived in a highly primitive fashion not unlike that of the native inhabitants of America before the "settlers" came. The long contact of these tribes with the Roman Empire seems to have had an effect on their beliefs, and their religion evolved over time, as such things do, picking up elements from Roman paganism as well as Greek.

When the Empire collapsed (due in part to Germani invaders from outside and insurrection from all those employed within Rome as mercenaries), there began a period known as the Migration, where many of the tribes rushed to conquer the former Roman lands. Around this time the Angles and the Saxons colonized England, and brought their religious practices there with them. On the continent the various Gothic tribes, and others such as the Vandals, settled various parts of Europe and commenced warring with each other. As this happened groups of warriors and free men united together under various princes, war-leaders, and emperors. (One of the things the Germani adopted from Rome was a love of grandiloquent titles). Nations of various degrees of stability were formed. This was the height of the heathen religious period, and saw a development of the religion's ideas and practices (fueled in part by the highly mobile nature of their societies, which assured a constant exposure to both new ideas and new perspectives on old ideas). It also saw the formation of a tradition of stories, myths, and history passed along orally.

The sixth century saw the beginnings of a strong attempt by the Christian church of the time to convert all those living in continental Europe and England. By the eighth century while England was still heathen the Christian church was a strong presence there. On the continent many tribes had already ceased most heathen practice. Sweden and Norway and Iceland were the countries to longest resist the Church. But eventually the people of Norway were forcibly converted, first by Olaf Tryggvason and then by that Olaf who was later titled Saint for his efforts at eradicating heathenism. They waged an unceasing war against the heathen faith, destroying idols, burning temples, defiling holy places, and killing those who resisted them. "St." Olaf was particularly enthusiastic in his pursuit of a Christian Norway. While he could be good and even fair-minded to those who obeyed him, with heathens he was - even by viking standards - ruthless. He tortured, maimed, and blinded them, drove and burned them from their homes. He doused them with pitch and lit them on fire. He was such a tyrant and a bloody-minded zealot that he became known to those he sought to eradicate as "Olaf the Lawbreaker". Iceland was colonized in great part by those who sought to escape these persecutions. (Though to be fair, Iceland was first colonized by those who sought to escape the tyranny of certain heathen monarchs.)

By the dawn of the eleventh century Iceland was in the middle of a great social turmoil. The Christian minority and the heathen majority refused to live under the same set of laws. This was slowly tearing the fabric of Icelandic society apart. One thing both the heathen and Christian Icelanders had in common was a strong sense of the societal bond. For this reason the schism that had formed was anathema to them all. A great Althing was called (the Icelandic legal assembly). The result of the Althing was that Iceland decided to adopt Christianity officially, in order to stop the eventual fragmentation of their country, as well as to ease growing economic sanctions placed on them by other, Christian countries, who would do no business with heathens. And by the twelfth century the last symbolic bastion of the heathen faith was gone, and Christians ruled in the old temple at Uppsala, in Sweden.

But of course this wasn't quite the end of the heathen faith. The peaceful nature of the Icelandic conversion helped preserve the heathen faith a while longer. Early churches were often attended on Sunday by those who still practiced the old heathen ways on other days. Much of the rituals, holy days, and nature of the early Icelandic church were thinly disguised heathen rituals, holy days, and nature. No record exists of how long the heathen faith continued to be practiced after this in secret. It seems likely that it survived, in one form or another, in at least a few isolated areas, for quite some time. It had been an oral tradition and enough of it was still around for Snorri to find and record, and Saemundr as well. In the sixteenth century the gods and wights of the old faith were still prayed to at least by magicians, as the Galdrabok, Huld Manuscript, etc. attest to. While it can be argued this is not likely a particularly deep form of religious practice it is religious practice nonetheless. The old faith quite obviously survived in mutated form as practices in folk traditions. All over Scandinavia there is a tradition, stretching back to heathen times, of the yearly ride of the Wild Hunt. Even to modern times there are traditions that it can only be heard, and not seen, and that when heard certain ritual behaviors must be engaged in. The Master of the hunt is still called Wode. Midsummer and May Day celebrations have always contained many old "traditional" practices that can be traced back to heathen religious observances. The Yule log dates back to heathen new year practices, and the Swedish Christmas tradition of baking a hog-shaped bread dates back to Frey's Yule sacrifice.

Sacrifices were still left to Odin, or his horse, under various names in the tradition of tying up the last bundle of rye from the harvest and leaving it in the field for them to ensure a good year to come, up to modern times. This too, while undoubtedly not thought of as such, is also religious practice; it's a sacrifice. And as a late as about 1750, so Benjamin Thorpe (noted scholar of Anglo-Saxon literature, law, and customs) tells us, a priest complained that many of his parishioners secretly attended a church that worshipped the alfs, headed by one of his parishioners. Thorpe also tells us that there were still altars being set up to the alfs, with sacrifices being offered, in his own time. At around the same time new traditions concerning Odin and Thor were forming. Thorpe gives a reference to recent worship of the old pagan gods, meaning their cults extended in fragmented form at least into the 18th century. The nineteenth century found an incantation in use in England that called upon Wod and Lok. The name Thor figured in a charm found used in rural America not that long ago. Do all these things point to a surviving tradition a la Margaret Murray? No. It was survival of an indirect sort, survival by inference, by custom, by story. But it was survival nonetheless. The old religion did not completely vanish.

Asatru is a reconstructionist religion. This means that Asatruar, when deciding any matter of faith, look to records such as the Eddas, the Sagas, and folk traditions of Scandinavian countries. Any new idea is compared to such sources, and if it does not match them it is discarded. In this we are like Hellenismos (the reconstructionist Greek pagan faith) and unlike such neopagan faiths as Wicca (a newly created religion done, in some degree or other, in a manner "like" a general mishmash of some of the pagan faiths). Asatru is not an Earth-based religion, though Jordh or Nerthus is a great and important goddess. But unlike the situation in Hellenismos, those who seek to reconstruct the paleopagan faith of the ancient Norse are left with very little source material to work from. And most of what we have was written decades or centuries after the major part of the heathen faith had passed out of existence, recorded by Christian scribes as an attempt at historical preservation. And this marks a difference of approach to research that defines many Asatruar. Some think that the date of the Eddas and Sagas, as well as their Christian authorship, invalidate them as sources of information, or at least restricts their usefulness to simply drawing upon general trends. They would also argue that at best the Eddas are a synthesis of ideas from over wide areas, and couldn't possibly represent the beliefs of any one people or person. This approach also doesn't tend to use folk traditions in Scandinavian countries as a source of information either, for similar reasons. This marks a particularly conservative approach to Asatru, and reliance is placed only on those very few sources of information that have been verified in multiple ways, archaeologically. This is a very safe way to reconstruct the faith of our paleopagan ancestors, in that few points of belief will be likely to be very dissimilar from what they held.

The other approach is to look at Asatru as an evolving tradition. Those holding this point of view would think our paleopagan predecessors would find it very odd, trying to reconstruct things as an exact replica of how they were in another world, 1000 years ago. Times, after all, change and people and religions change with them. This is the only conclusion possible to draw from history. This approach to Asatru sees the survival of the faith in folk tradition and Christian history as a survival. The religion had changed before, in point of fact, when it came into contact with Greek and Roman religions. This is part of the evolution of any tradition. This point of view sees the Eddas as a synthesis of ideas to be sure, but a form representative of those ideas nonetheless. This is the point of view I favor myself, particularly because I think that what we have for information as it stands is too little. To draw from too restricted a pool of information is to worship in an incomplete and unbalanced way, which is definitely not something our predecessors did. (For one thing, goddess lore is almost entirely lacking.) Though to be sure I know a good many solid Asatruar who are more of the first sort; I certainly don't mean to disparage anyone's mode of practice.

Since the time of the Conversion many new stories of the gods and spirits arose for a variety of reasons. Sometimes this was because their worship had not entirely died out in a certain place, sometimes this was because folk beliefs were strong enough to resist entirely the changes wrought by the new religion. Modern Asatruar often draw upon these stories, where they are known, to supplement the existing lore found in the Eddas and Sagas. The purpose of this book is to collect many of these stories together in one place, such as with the ancient Eddas. It should not be thought that the collection is exhaustive; there are likely many more stories to be found with diligent research. But I felt it necessary to make what beginning in this area I could, and publish what stories I could find.

* * *

As a word first on the nature of ancient heathen practice would not be entirely out of place, I have included the following into this introduction:

The element of ancient heathen worship that was, arguably, of greatest importance to the average person was worship of the spirits of the land, trees, rocks, rivers and such natural features.

The land-vaettir, or land-wights, are the spirits of the land. The land-vaettir are sometimes pictured as Trolls, living below the ground in mounds which are hence called vaette-houer. They are also sometimes pictured as women, or as young boys. In their more unbalanced and harmful aspects, the land-wights are seen as thurses, jotunns, etins, and trolls, and are the powers of frost, and fire, and storm, and avalanche. In Ulfliot's law the dragon prows of viking ships had to be removed before sighting home, lest they frighten the land-wights. When Egil Skallagrimsson wanted to remove King Eirik from Norway he directed a curse at the land-wights of Norway, to give them no rest until they drove him out. They were also sometimes seen as identical with the huldra-folk, the people of the goddess Huldra. They are a kind of fairy that looks like a beautiful woman in every detail, but for a cow's tail. Other huldra-folk are called wood-wives, and look like beautiful women from the front, but from behind can be seen to be hollow wood. The vitality of the land-wights is the vitality of their land. As such, worship given to the land-wights, to ensure good harvest and prosperity was an important part of old heathen religious practice.

Practically identical with the land-wights are the alfar, or alfs. There are several types of alf. The ljossalfar, or light-alfs, are capricious yet potentially beneficial powers that were ruled by the god Frey in Ljossalfheim. They sometimes stole into human dwellings at night and knotted horses' tails, and rode them. They might beset lone travelers and shoot darts at them, or lead them astray. They might also lead them home. The beauty and rapture of their music and dance could sweep a mortal up into irresistible dance that ended only in death. They might also aid certain other households, and perform small chores about the house at night, such as sweeping or baking bread. (This is where the fairy tale of the shoemaker and the elves comes from.) The alfs might be propitiated, and as such could offer good luck, assistance in times of trouble, good harvest and the like. The ceremony of propitiation was known as the Alf-blot, and involved leaving out a bowl of milk or honey. Certain alfs were worshipped as household divinities and their images were carved on doorposts of the households they were attached to. These household gods sometimes traveled with a family, showing them where to settle as colonists in new lands by having their images thrown over the side of the ship, and followed ashore. Many alfs were tied to certain plants, such as trees, and would die if the plant were killed. Alfs were often said to live underground, in mounds, and might kidnap human beings they fell in love with or just took a passing fancy to.

The Svartalfar, or black-alfs, were also called dwarfs. They lived deep under ground, and their home is Svartalfheim. Sometimes their habitation is said to be in stones, and for this reason certain stones are holy, and the dwarf within is worshipped as the spirit of the land around the stone. Dwarfs are great miners, and craftsmen, and the works of certain dwarfs comprise some of the dearest held of the gods' treasures. They were also sometimes worshipped as household divinities. In truth, the distinction between light-alfs and dark-alfs is somewhat arbitrary, and not completely accurate. There was a lot of overlap in how they were looked at. Dwarfs are often highly motivated by self interest, and are little given to interacting with other peoples. Many dwarf names have something to do with death, or the dead, or with speaking to the dead. Thus the dwarfs were also connected with worship of the dead, and possibly with the practice of necromancy. Sometimes dwarfs are said to turn to stone if exposed to sunlight. They seem to be also somewhat identical with Trolls and Kobolds (a form of spirit associated with both mines and households). There are dwarf names that refer to the waxing and waning moons, and the four cardinal points of the compass are named for the dwarfs that stand there. Thus the worship of the dwarfs also was related to the worship of the subordinate powers.

Dokkalfar, or dark-alfs, is a more ambiguous term that seems to have been used in a number of ways. Sometimes it seems to refer to the dwarfs, and sometimes to alfs who dwell in forests, and sometimes to the dead, ancestors who dwell in their burial mounds and continue to look after the welfare of their families. As such they are somewhat synonymous with the drow, or draugar, who are the dead (either in the form of spectres or animate corpses). This confusion of alfs or landwights with the dead is typical of many Indo-European societies. Thus ancestor worship is blended with worship of the alfs/land-wights.

A related aspect of the old heathen faith was the worship of the disir. A dis is simply a mythic female being, and such were considered to be attached to certain family lines, or certain houses, or even to certain individuals. A dis might be a dead female ancestor, or a minor goddess, or an alf, or a troll, or even a valkyrie. A dis attached to an individual was referred to as a fylgja (which term could also describe an animal spirit attached to an individual). A fylgja is something like a tutelary spirit, an attendant. They offer protection, but also bring death when it is time. They were usually unseen for the duration of an individual's life, appearing only as a harbinger of death. But certain individuals might develop a deeper relationship with them, and learn and benefit from their aid. A dis approached for aid in fortune-telling was referred to as a spadis. The holy festivals in their honor were called disablots. One such was the first night of the Yule holiday, called Mother-night.

A spirit akin to the fylgja is also known, called the thusbet, which is a sort of dark totemic spirit. A thusbet also follows each mortal, as a fylgja does, and looks ever to his death or undoing.

The worship of land-wights, alfs, ancestors, and personal spirits was one of the most important parts of old heathen worship. It was perhaps an even larger part of the average heathen's life than worship of the gods was. Some might center their worship around their own personal spirits then, or around a local holy rock. The spirits of prominent local rivers and mountains were also much venerated. These things, as well as the personal relationship one might develop with a particular god (called a patron) lend Asatru, both ancient and modern, a highly individual flavor. One person's form of worship was and is not necessarily much like his neighbor's, though both were and are aspects of the same system.

The other major aspect of ancient heathen religion was worship of the gods.

Odin: Odin is a god of many things. I mean that in the sense that he presides over them, or is the cause, or effector of them. Chief amongst them, perhaps, is death. Odin is the psychopomp, the ferryman who conducts souls from the land of the living to the land of the dead. He is the one who hands out death. As such he is the one who apportions victory in battle, as the one who controls death also controls the victory. From this he is also god of battle itself, and we see this function in the war-strategies he gifts certain of his chosen humans with, as well as in the berserkergang, the internal-style martial art his devotees fought with. He is god of poetry, and is the apportioner of inspiration. He is god of wine (and probably many if not all mind-altering substances). He is the god of seidh-craft. (A vaguely shamanic sort of practice. However, *not* identifiable with shamanism.) He is god of sex, in that where Thor boasts of jotuns slain, Odin boasts of women slept with. (This is sex for sex's own sake, rather than having to do with relationships.) These last two things also come together in a third way. Seidh practice may have involved various cross-gendered practices, such as cross-dressing or passive homosexuality. (This is not a certain thing. There are arguments both ways about it. But male seidh practitioners were often referred to as seidhberendur, and berendur was a coarse term in Old Norse for female genitalia, and was used to refer to homosexual men, amongst other things.) Thus Odin can also be seen as god of the transgendered of various kinds.

There is something that all of these things have in common. Death is the destruction of the physical self. Battle is the transcendence of the self in the moment, as seen in the berserkergang. Poetry writing in particular, and inspiration in general involve the loss of the self as it is caught up in the information coming in from the outside. Wine brings about loss of the self through dulling of the hugr. Sex is loss of the self in another, and in the moment. And seidh involves spiritual death and rebirth in a different form. Transgendering of course is loss of gender-self. All of Odin's functions at heart relate to the same thing. He is a god of the loss of the self, the death of the ego, in all the many ways that can happen.

Odin fulfills a god's role found in certain other religions as well. He is much like the Celtic Lugh, as well as a sort of combination of Hermes and Dionysos in Greek mythology. He is like the Slavic Volos as well, the Baltic Velinas, and possibly the Hindu Vata.

It seems that Odin began as the ancient Germanic god Woden, or Wotan. This is not *precisely* the same god. You could say their minnis (memories, subconscious natures) are the same but their hugrs (conscious minds, personalities) are, while related, a little different. This is because a god's hugr is affected by the way his people perceive him. Woden was originally a god of storm, and of the Wild Hunt (the train of the dead who ride through the night sky during the winter half of the year). He was a wanderer of the nine worlds, and was a creature of the Out-Worlds, the wild dangerous places outside the habitations of men. His aspect as Lord of Death was primary. He was a bloodthirsty god, completely uncivilized, and people were often sacrificed to him. (Though these were mostly condemned criminals and prisoners of war.) As Adam of Bremen said, "Woden; that means fury."

But this form was not the only one the god took. It seems that at some point, as the worship of Woden spread on the outside of Germany, that the perception of the god changed. He became known as the father of the runes, and as such became the father of magic. He became associated with the practice of seidh as well, possibly through contact of the ancient Norse with the Saami, a highly "shamanic" people. As these things happened, he began to take over many of the functions of and nature of Tiwaz, the Germanic god Snorri gives us as Tyr. He took over his position as All-Father, and largely seems to have replaced him as god of war. He became more worshipped by the aristocratic classes. He became more civilized (though at heart he was still drighten of draugs, lord of the dead), and those who pursued the intellectual arts appealed to him. Human sacrifice played a much lesser part of his worship, and in some areas was ceased altogether. In this form he was viewed as an exemplary model for those who would obtain wisdom. He was god of eloquence, a law-giver, king, and judge. He also came to be worshipped as a god of crops, of the fertility of the land. In this form he was known as Odhinn (pronounced Oth-in, where the th is soft as in "the").

The modern spelling of "Odin" is due primarily to researchers' ignoring the distinction between the Icelandic letter for the soft th and the Icelandic letter for d. This is the way the name is rendered in modern times, in myth and folklore. For this reason many modern worshippers are returning to the spelling Odhinn. I would disagree with this practice, for the reason that the god we know now as Odin is not precisely Odhinn, just as Odhinn is not precisely the same as Woden. Minni is the same, hugr is different. For one thing, when the god was last worshipped, the world and his worshippers were both very different. They did not see things as people today see them. Exposing infants was still regarded as a necessity during famine. Prisoners of war were routinely executed. One had little if any moral debt to strangers. Going viking, which included murder, rape, and theft, was considered acceptable. And for another thing, the knowledge we have of Odin, coming from such sources as myths heard in childhood and scholarly works by modern authors, is changed by the long tradition of literature and folklore that has preserved the stories. A whole period of Germanic Romanticism produced works of art, poetry, opera, and more that painted and repainted Odin in different ways, as times changed. It could be argued that this is a corruption of Odin's nature, but as the changes are sprung from the evolution of the Germanic cultures, I think it much more appropriate to think of them as the way in which Odin himself has evolved.

The Odin of modern times continues the process begun in the transition from Woden to Odhinn. The intellectual is much more pronounced. He is god of the runes, and of seidh. He is god of death, but the psychopomp aspect, as well as the seidh-related aspect of death and rebirth are emphasized. He is still god of battle, but as the culture of the warrior is gone, and warriors with them, he is now more a god of the martial arts. Sacrifices to him are still of blood, but it is the blood of he who does the sacrificing. He has become a god of the individual, and individual development, especially those who seek wisdom and personal power. (At the same time he is a god of society, as the chief of all the gods.) He is seen as a god of transcendence, as his death upon the World Tree relates, as does the story of the sacrifice of Mimir's well. In this way he is god of the berserk and seidh-man both. He is the giver of inspiration and he who overcomes adversity. And he is still the mad leader of the Wild Hunt, and the Grim Reaper.

Thor: The strongest god, son of Odin and Jordh, the Earth. He rules over the realm of Thrudheim, and his mansion is named Bilskirnir. He drives a chariot pulled by two flying goats, Tanngniost and Tanngrisnir. He is god of the rain (and as such is also a god of the crops), and the thunder, and the lightning. He is the protector of gods and men alike, and is the eternal enemy of the jotunns (giants), thurses, etins, and trolls, who seek ever to destroy the lands of gods and men. In fact Thor has a piece of whetstone imbedded in his forehead from a particularly great battle with a giant armed with a whetstone club. Tales told of Thor often involve his travels to the lands of these beings, for purposes of adventure and slaughter. A companion in his travels is often Loki, and there is a mystery in this, for Thor is the only power Loki really respects (fears) and as such is the natural counterbalance to him. (This also works in reverse as well, for Loki's sharp wits and wily ways are often of benefit to Thor as well, and serve in ways brute strength cannot.) Thor's wife is Sif, who is looked at as a goddess of the crops. Thor possesses three chief treasures: the hammer Mjollnir, iron gauntlets, and a magic girdle. The hammer almost never misses. Nothing can stand before it and it returns to its wielder's hand after it has been thrown. It is the lightning. The iron gauntlets are needed to handle the great heat and power of the hammer and the magic girdle doubles the strength of its wearer. Thor is often pictured in modern sources as slow of wit, something of a redneck of a god. This shows a certain lack of understanding of him. He is a very wise and intelligent being. After all, he was able to keep a dwarf he could not kill for social reasons in conversation about deep cosmic matters for an entire night, until the sun arose. It is just that Thor's wisdom is a practical kind of wisdom, rather than the showy kind seen in Odin. Thor was perhaps the most popular of the gods, and while Odin's people are jarls (noblemen) or wargs (outlaws), Thor's people are carls, freemen, the ordinary people who loved him best. Thor is god of farmers, and common folk, as well as fighters. One would pray to Thor for strength, and protection, and for land, and for rain. It is also said that mere mention of Thor's name aloud can cause the god to take notice, and suddenly appear.

Tyr: Another of the chief Aesir, he is said to be the bravest. A person who exceeds all others is thus called Ty-brave. He is also a very wise god, and so the highly intelligent are called Ty-wise. He is identical to Teiwaz, described by Tacitus in his study of the Germani. As such it seems he was the original sky-father, and ruler of the pantheon, and god of war before Odin took over these attributes. He is a god of social order, and of justice. He would be prayed to for skill in combat, for it was an art he was most skilled in. He would also be prayed to for victory in legal matters, though this is usually a matter of praying for strictly interpreted justice. He is not a god of peace and is said to be one who is not known to settle quarrels amongst men. He is a god of honor, sticking strictly to the word given. Tyr's men and Odin's men are famous for not seeing things eye-to-eye.

Njord: He dwells in Noatun, by the sea, and rules the course of the wind, stills the ocean, and quenches fire. He is prayed to by fishermen and sailors. He is a Vanir, and is said to be so rich that those who desire a superfluity of wealth also pray to him. He was married to Skadhi. His sister is Nerthus, and he may have been the original male deity sacrificed to her yearly. They are the parents also of Frey and Freya.

Baldur: Odin's son by Frigga. His name means "warrior" and he seems to have epitomized the best aspects of the warrior class. He is the most fair of aspect, the most beautiful god. He is one of the wisest and most eloquent, and none are able to pervert his judgments. He is friendly in nature, and no impure thing is able to enter his realm of Breidhablik. He is married to Nanna. He was killed by a plot of Loki's (as part of a deeper plot of Odin's to ensure the continuity of the world past Ragnarok) who guided the hand of a blind god to hurl at him the one weapon that could kill him. He was then forced to remain in Hel by another trick of Loki's. It is notable that Baldur goes to Hel and is then forced to remain there, for it is the one place that will be safe from the ravages of Ragnarok. Indeed, because of this the Voluspa tells us that after Ragnarok Baldur will return and take the dead Odin's place. Every treachery of Loki's ends up ultimately to the benefit of men and gods both, for this is Loki's nature. Because of this, and because Baldur goes to Hel rather than to his father's own realm of Valhalla, which would seem much more natural, most Asatruar see it as part of Odin's eternal struggle to stave off Ragnarok, and to preserve something through it, by sacrificing his own son for the benefit of all the worlds. (Some scholars thus try to see Baldur in a very Christ-like light, but this is error. The sacrifice is coincidental and has more to do with reincarnation doctrine than redemption.) And note: *Baldur is not a solar deity.* There is a lot of misinformation floating around out there about this point, perpetrated mostly by scholars overly influenced by Frazer and his like who got "solar deity happy" and tried to see every male deity as a sun god. But Baldur's death and eventual return is clearly spoken of as part of a world-cycle, not a year-cycle.

Heimdall: Called sometimes an Ase, sometimes a Van. Said to be a son of Odin and nine mothers. He is also called the White God, or the Bright God, for he is said to shine. He is the watchman of the gods, and stays mostly in his home Himinbjorg, next to the Bridge Bifrost, the way to Asgard, which he guards. He is a most faithful watchman, and is often rained on. He needs less sleep than a bird, can hear the grass grow all the way in Midgard, as well as the wool on sheep. He has a horn called Gjallarhorn, which he will sound when the giant-hordes approach and Ragnarok draws nigh. There are also scholarly arguments that say certain sources tell of a sacrifice Heimdall made similar to Odin's, where he sacrificed an ear for a drink from Mimir's well, which is how he got his hearing. This, if true, is such a close parallel with Odin that it may be that Heimdall is a well-developed heiti of Odin's, that has become an hypostasis. Heimdall, under the name Rig, also fathered the three races of man (thralls, or slaves, carls, or freemen, and jarls, or nobles). As such he is also a god of social order. He is also the only god other than Odin who is said to teach the runes. He would be called on by guards, police, and such like. He would also be called on by runic students as well as those who seek transcendence (as god of Bifrost, and possibly as god of social-climbing).

Bragi: The god of eloquence. He is also known as a patron of the art of poetry. From him comes the rite of Bragi's cup, where those performing the rite take turns to speak proudly of their accomplishments. We get the word bragging from this, but the old Norse did not seem to necessarily see o'erweening ego in this practice. It seemed more their point of view that a person should be able to be honest in all things, to speak poorly of him or herself when deserved and to speak well of him or herself when deserved. False modesty seems to be looked at more as a form of hypocrisy and lying, as well as denoting a weak ego that needs a certain kind of feeding.

Hod: This name also means "warrior", and he is very strong. But he is also blind, and it was his hand that Loki guided to the killing of Baldur. Hod was afterwards killed, and resides with Baldur in Hel.

Vidar: The Silent God. Also the god of the really big shoe. He is the son of Odin and the giantess Grid. He never speaks, and has a giant thick-soled shoe he got from his mother. This is made from the scraps that are discarded when humans make shoes and is continually being added to. The shoe is so that when Odin is killed by the Fenris wolf at Ragnarok Vidar can avenge his father by tearing the wolf's jaw off by bracing against it with the shoe. Thus all who love the Aesir must take care to discard scraps from shoe-making, rather than saving them for future use.

Ullr: God of the winter. He is the son of Sif and the stepson of Thor. He is god of archery and snowshoeing and skiing. All those sports and arts of the wintertime are his. He is also god of single combat, and those who go into it should call upon him. He might also be viewed as god of those things requiring precision. He is sometimes the consort of the goddess Holle, or Huldra.

Forseti: Son of Baldur and Nanna, he dwells in the mansion Glitner, and he settles all quarrels. No one, god or man, knows better judgments than his.

Loki: Technically Loki is a giant, but Snorri refers to him as one of the twelve Aesir whose natures are divine. Also, he is spoken of as a blood-brother of Odin. Because of this, whenever a toast is given to Odin one is also given to Loki. Those who understand this should offer a separate toast to Loki after offering one to Odin but technically the deal Odin and Loki struck means that a toast to Odin IS also a toast to Loki. He is a god of chaos, and change for change's own sake. In its lighter form this means he is a god of mischief (I have known Loki's men who say that in this form he is very much like The Red Guy on the cartoon Cow and Chicken). In its darker form this means he is god of destruction and harm, almost a Norse Satan. But looking at him purely as this is a mistake, as it is only one extreme of his being. Loki is most holy, and is a necessary part of the pantheon. This is a great mystery, and needs much study to understand it. Loki is a trickster, and often betrays his friends. But actually reading his myths, every time he does things, things work out in such a way that it is ultimately to the benefit of gods and men both. This is Loki's nature. He also gets his friends out of as much trouble as he gets them into. He is the chaos and destruction necessary to preserve creation any length of time. A created thing must inevitably be destroyed, ended by the very same law that gave it form. Fresh new governments become entrenched bureaucracies. Customs become chains. Many of the best treasures of the gods, things the gods have that are needed for their safety and that of the worlds were derived from some betrayal or custom-breaking of Loki's that none of the other gods could do, for reasons of honor or politics. A woman of

Loki once said that he is the force that breaks the dam that blocks up the stream, stagnating the water and killing the life within. Loki is that which destroys that which needs destroying. He is god of laughter, and a prime function those who have Loki as a patron can serve is to never let anyone go too long without laughing. Another is to make sure no one becomes too complacent or impressed with themselves, and as such should take example from the poem "The Flyting of Loki". This is not a comfortable function for either the Loki's man or the recipients of his flyting, but the health of a kindred can be greatly benefited from an integrated relationship with its Lokian, if it is fortunate enough to have one. Many kindreds either refuse to look at priests of Loki as real priests, or if they do they tend to look down on them but in this I feel they fail to understand either Loki's nature or the Asatru world view of the holy. It should also be noted that there seems to have never been a priesthood of Loki's amongst the paleopagans. This is a modern phenomenon. Loki is also said to be bound underneath the earth, in torture, to await Ragnarok, in punishment for his part in Baldur's death. But modern priests and priestesses of Loki, while acknowledging its truth, say that this can only be an hypostasis of Loki, for clearly he must still be in the world, as laughter, mischief, and chaos are. Loki might be called upon for laughter, or for mischief, or for saying those truths that are too unpleasant for others to say. He should be called upon for cleverness. He has been called the god of dirty tricks. He is also sometimes called upon by telemarketers. Loki's worshippers have much in common with Discordians. But be warned: every Loki's man I know says that it is an extremely difficult path, and that Loki's attention can be quite painful. I know two Loki's men who swear the proper sacrifice to Loki is either an alcoholic drink, a peanut butter and jelly sandwich, or a cup of coffee.

Frey: Frey means "Lord" and is more of a title than a name. The real name of this god may have been Ing, which means "Hero". Frey is a Van, and son of Njord. He may actually be synonymous with this god, and been the god sacrificed to Nerthus during certain of her rituals. (Two separate traditions might have given the god different names, and when the traditions came together again it was decided they were father and son.) He is the god who taught agriculture to men, and is known as "God of the Earth". He is prayed to in matters concerning crops, and virility. His quest for the giantess Gerdhr, the Earth, cost him his sword. For this reason he will be forced to fight at Ragnarok with a stag's antler, and it will cost him his life. He may be identical with a series of semi-mythical kings known as Frodhi, and as such legends about them may be taken as legends about him. But I have not yet talked with enough Frey's men to make up my own mind on this matter. Frey is lord of peace, and plenty, and good harvest. He owns a marvelous ship that can fly and folds up so small as to fit in his pocket. (It is thus possibly a symbol of virility, a phallic symbol.) The horse is sacred to Frey. He rides upon a golden-bristled boar, who may be the sun, which would actually make Frey a solar deity.

Frigga: Queen of the gods, wife of Odin, ruler of his household. Her habitation is called Fensalir. She is a patron of marriage. She is said to be most wise, and to know the destiny of all men. She keeps silent on these matters to all but Odin, whom she advises. She has definite interests in Midgard and can get into power struggles with Odin over just how things should get resolved. In these struggles Odin seems to inevitably lose. She also seems to have a rivalry with some of Odin's other wives and lovers.

Freya: Sister of Frey, daughter of Njord and Nerthus. Freya is not so much a name as a title, and means Lady. She is called Vanadis, and is a dis of the Vanir. She may be identical with the goddess Nerthus, in the way Frey might be identical with Njord. Her realm is Folkvang, her hall Sessrymnir. She is goddess of seidh, and taught that art to Odin (while learning galdr from him). She is also a goddess of war and is called Valfreya, Lady of the Slain. This may refer to the fact that she receives half those warriors slain in battle (getting first choice, even before Odin). This may also mean she is head of the Valkyries, Odin's warrior women. She is goddess of the Earth, and the crops. She is a goddess of fertility, and sex, and passion. Part of her worship in pagan times involved writing erotic poetry dedicated to her. It was said to so inflame the passions that even in pagan times it was illegal for a man to read Freya's poetry to an unmarried woman. This poetry was the reason that Christians were so thorough in eradicating any of Freya's lore. She is in many ways a female form of Odin (though not a female side of Odin). She possesses a falcon's plumage cloak, which turns its wearer into a falcon. She is married to Odin under the name of Odhr (though "married" might have been a Christian term, used because a scribe was uncomfortable with the idea of a consort, which seems to more accurately describe her relationship to Odin). But Odhr's wandering nature sometimes stirs him to leave her, and wander the worlds. When he does this, she seeks ever after him, in her chariot drawn by cats, weeping tears that become gold. For this reason gold is sacred to her. It seems likely that she was a birch goddess. She is one of the two goddesses the giants are always trying to abduct. She has a magic necklace, which is called Brisingamen, which may be identical, symbolically, with the whole earth. The "Valentine's heart" was originally a symbol of Freya, and actually represents sex more than romantic love (it is a representation of the vulva). The ladybug (freyabug) is also a symbol of her.

Idunn: The wife of Bragi. She tends the youth-giving apples the gods must always eat in order to remain alive and young. (The Norse knew that all things die; men, worlds, and gods alike.) Her dwelling is in Brunnakr, and she is the other goddess the giants always seek to kidnap.

Sif: Thor's wife. Goddess of the crops. She was said to have beautiful hair, which Loki is said to have cut off. But cutting off a woman's hair was a Norse punishment for adultery, and many scholars agree that this was a gentler way Christian scribes recorded the myth. They say it is quite likely Loki slept with Sif, and Thor found out, and things were not right again until Loki got the dwarfs to make her a new head of hair. This would likely be a yearly cycle, where Sif is Thor's wife in the summer, and her hair is the plant life of the world. In the winter she becomes Loki's lover, and is shorn of her hair, and the plants of the world die.

Hel: Daughter of Loki, queen of one of the realms of the dead, also called Hel. Hel (the goddess) is half living flesh, fair to behold, and half decaying corpse. This is because she wears the two faces death has for humans, the fair and the terrifying. Hel (the realm) is the polar opposite of Valhalla in many ways. As Valhalla is the height of activity, Hel is the height of inertia, a dark, still, resting.

Saga: Goddess of history. Wife of Odin. Her home is Sokvabek, where cool waves murmur, and she and Odin while away many a pleasant hour there.

Skadhi: A giantess, daughter of Thiassi, whom the gods killed. She went to the gods seeking vengeance, but Loki prevented this by making her agree to drop her claim if he could make her laugh then tying his balls to the beard of a goat (rightly judging she was a wight who could appreciate the humor of pain). She became a goddess by marrying Njord, but they were unable to live together, as he preferred the sea and she the frozen mountains. She is said to have later married Ullr, with whom she had more in common. She is a goddess of hunting, and skiing, and the winter.

Gefjon: Goddess of virgins. Young women who die virgins go to her. She is not necessarily a virgin herself.

Eir: Goddess of healers.

Fulla: Handmaid of Frigga.

Gna: Messenger of Frigga.

Hlin: Guardian of those humans Frigga wishes to protect.

Lofn: Goddess of lovers. She brings them together, even in difficult circumstances.

Vor: She hears the vows of lovers and punishes those who break faith.

Syn: A goddess who guards the doors of the hall. She also protects those destined to lose a court case because of another's perjury.

Snotra: Goddess of elegance and manners. She is very wise.

Ostara: Goddess of spring.

Bertha: The White Lady, a birch goddess. She is supposed to dwell in a hollow mountain, and the souls of unborn children were in her keeping. She is patron of spinning and every Yule she went to every house where this art was practiced. Good spinners were rewarded with the goddess' own flax, but bad spinners, or those who failed to honor the goddess by eating enough of the right cakes at Yule were punished by her. She was also supposed to travel the world during Yule, followed sometimes by the dead or the souls of the unborn children and tradition credits her with leaving gifts for good children and with either leaving birch twigs to punish the bad ones or to take them away with her in a sack.

Perchta: A birch goddess. She was a patron of spinning, and led the Wild Hunt during the winter. Some of her worshippers comprised a mystery cult, and were called Perchten. They became possessed by the dead, or by the goddess herself, in a ritual apparently related to her procession as leader of the Wild Hunt. She seems almost certainly to be another name for Bertha. Both names are derived from the name for birch.

Huldra or **Holle**: Another birch goddess. She is patron of household chores and duties, such as spinning. Her realm is sometimes found by going down a well. She is helpful to young women who perform well their cleaning and chores, and punishes those who don't. She also is said to lead the Wild Hunt and during the winter, is said by some to be the consort of Ullr. She is leader of the huldrafolk, a sort of land-wight.

Nerthus, or **Eartha**, or **Jordh**: Tacitus describes her as living in a holy grove. Twice a year she is supposed to leave the grove and go on a procession about the land, bringing prosperity and good harvest. These processions take place at the beginning of the summer half of the year and at the beginning of the winter half. At the end of the ritual the priest leading the procession brought the wagon the goddess symbolically rode around in and her holy symbol, back to the grove. Slaves accompanied him and ritually they washed everything. The slaves were then killed, either by drowning or strangling. Some scholars hold that the slaves might represent a male fertility deity. It was recorded that during her procession was a time of peace. No one took up arms, and there was no quarreling.

* * *

It was no easy decision to determine how to present these stories. I wished to avoid simply listing them one after the other, as that would be too dry and pedantic. I wished also to avoid putting too much of myself into the Edda, as writing an extensive narrative framework would require. So I chose to emulate Snorri and provide the very barest of bones as a narrative framework. Additionally I used a character and a setting based upon Snorri's original narrative in the Gylfaginning. I hope in this way to provide a connection, as it were, to the faith of the ancients, in the last time period the holy stories were collected.

-Wayland Skallagrimsson

New Edda

Gangleri Gylfi was a man living in the country of Sweden. Of him it is said that he was a descendent of those kings who once ruled Sweden, and also that he was a wise and learned man. He once gave an old vagrant man money for food and clothing, and to thank him for his generosity the old man told him stories of the ancient gods, the Aesir and the Vanir, the alfar, and the disir. Gangleri was quite amazed at what he heard, and desired to know whether the old gods yet lived. So mighty and powerful did they seem he thought it might be so. So he set off wandering into the world to find an answer to his questions.

Now the Aesir are wise, and have the gift of prophecy, and they saw his movements. So they, and one of them in particular, set things up in such a fashion that Gangleri's steps were led inevitably to a great sprawling mansion. Standing outside the great edifice was a smith, a giant of a man, hard at work at a forge, striking glowing iron with a giant hammer. "Enter my house, traveler, and be refreshed," offered the smith. Gangleri entered.

Once inside Gangleri saw that the house was a maze. No

sooner had he rounded a corner, it seemed, than he became hopelessly lost. He passed libraries, drawing rooms, trophy rooms, work rooms, and never did he find another living soul, nor the door he came in by, nor any other. He passed by busts, and statues, and display cases of fossils trapped in stone. He passed by a meteor in a glass display case mounted on a stand, and a great oil painting, half the size of the wall, of a mighty lightning bolt striking a remote mountain-top. At length he came into a sitting room wherein were three magnificent chairs, like thrones, set before a roaring fire. In each chair was seated a man. The man on the left introduced himself as High, and the one in the middle named himself Just-As-High, and the one on the right bore the name of Third. They offered Gangleri food and drink, and the run of the house. Gangleri said that he would rather first find if there was any learned man about, for he sought the answers to certain questions. The three put it to him that they could answer between them any questions he might ask. He told them he wished to learn all that he might of the ancient gods, whether they were still in existence and what they might have been doing since last they were heard of.

Then spoke Gangleri: "What of Thor? What were things like with him from the time of the Conversion 'till generations came to be and the human race was multiplied?"

Just-As-High said: "At the time of the Conversion Thor was the defender of the Aesir and the Vanir, of the elves and dwarves, and of the true men and women. To the people of those days the struggle of the people of the Cross against those of the heathen lands was called the struggle between the White Christ and the Red Thor. Though in sooth not all those he protected properly appreciated him."

Then High spoke thusly: "The Saxons once had an oak tree of prodigious girth, and called it the Oak of Donar, which is the name by which they called Thor. They held the tree sacred to him, and held council under the protection of its branches."

Then spoke Just-As-High: "One named Boniface came to the Saxons, with word of his god, who was desirous that all other men should follow the same god. When he saw that the Saxons put much by the oak he was resolved to fell it."

And Third said: "Though he was alone, and surrounded by men who called themselves friends of Thor, not one of them tried to stop this direct insult to their god. They had decided to let Thor take care of his own, if such was his will. And they were doubtful, in their hearts, that Thor was stronger than the god of the stranger, and they mistrusted their red-bearded protector."

And Gangleri asked: "What happened then?"

High replied: "What do you think might happen? Saddened by the falsity of his friends, and seeing that no one around would try to prevent this affront, he took matters into his own hands. Calling up a sudden thunderstorm (for thunder is his province) he felled the tree himself with a mighty gale, before Boniface could so much as touch it. And when it fell it was split into four quarters of exactly equal size, that none might doubt it was a matter of divine work. And for many a year he came no more to that country."

Gangleri said: "Was that the end of Thor then?"

To which Just-As-High rejoined: "Not at all. There were still some few who held their troth. I am minded to tell of Torbjonn, the god-image of Thor belonging to a family who kept the faith of their fathers many centuries after the old ways were gone. In Vradal there was a farm called Flatland. Many years ago Thor himself had paid a visit there, and sat at the highseat. The family kept a god-image of him in that place, a stump large and thick at the base of it to keep it from falling over. They named the image Torbjonn, which means 'Thor's Bear'. It had no arms or legs, but a carving of a human head sat atop it. Its eyes were filled with tin. The top of the head was flat, and it was the custom of that family to place a bowl of beer atop it for an offering whenever the beer-bowl was out, as when there were guests. In the light of the fire the tin of his eyes flashed and glinted, and the beer-bowl on his head looked like a war helmet, and all-in-all he was a very impressive image."

And High added: "Their custom was that one of the guests would take the bowl from Torbjonn's head and hail him by saying "Good year, Torbjonn!" and take a drink from the bowl. He would then pass it around the table where everyone present would hail him in like fashion."

To which Third said: "Now there was a Christian priest named Otto Stoud, who one day approached the farmer of his day, who was named Anund Flatland. He asked him to destroy the heathen image. Anund refused, saying that it was a part of his family, and reassured the priest that he had never used it, nor had his father. Old Anund got his will and there Torbjonn remained. But one day when guests were present something went wrong, and Torbjonn ended up with an axe stuck in his head. It is not known if the stroke was deliberate, but most there present asserted it was. At this Anund knew bad events were in store, for he respected still the power he knew was in the image."

Gangleri asked: "And did anything come of it?"

High answered him: "Sometime later a strange fire flared up on the roofs of the houses of the farm for no reason anyone could see. And just as suddenly it went out. People said that this was surely a warning of ill fate to come, and that Torbjonn would avenge the injury done him. But the farmer had a daughter, by the name of Jorunn, who had always been friendly with Torbjonn and would talk to him. She prayed to him, and asked mercy and forgiveness. Torbjonn promised her that for her sake he should spare the farm for so long as she lived, and she knew prosperity and riches from then until the end of her days. But when she died the entire farm was consumed in a great fire, and Torbjonn with it. And that was the last of the worship of Thor in the North in those days. When he saw himself abandoned and ridiculed, and the last person who cared for him was dead, he himself lit his own funeral pyre. In that way he was his reputation worthy."

Gangleri lowered his head for a moment in thought. Raising it he queried: "And did no one else hold true to Thor through all those years? Were the farmers of Flatland his only friends?"

Third said: "No. They were not. In the days of whaling, long centuries after the Conversion, a Dutch ship departed Amsterdam, for the whaling grounds near Greenland. Foul weather drove them off their course and they were no longer sure of their heading. Lights on a nearby shore, as of a great fire burning there, drew the attention of the crew, many of whom were from Bohuslan in Holland."

Just-As-High added: "Some of the sailors, amongst which was one of them from Bohuslan, were seized with a desire to visit the shore, and perchance get their bearings. They therefore took a ship's boat and rowed to the shore. Upon approaching the fire they found seating by it an old man warming his hands. Before they even had a chance to speak, he asked them from whence they hailed. 'From Holland,' said the Bohuslaning. 'But from what place art thou thyself?' pressed the old man. 'From Safve on Hisingen' was the sailor's answer. 'Art acquainted with Thorsby?' came the next question. 'Yes' was its response. 'Dost know where the Ulfveberg is?' 'Yes, I have often passed it, for there is a direct way through there from Gothenborg to Marstrand.'"

High: "The old man then asked 'Do the great stones and earthen mounds still stand in their places?' 'Yes,' was his answer, 'all but one stone which is ready to fall.' 'Tell me further, dost thou know where Glosshed's altar is, and whether it is still safe and sound?' When the sailor told him that it was not, the old man asked of him a favor. 'Wilt thou convince the people in Thorsby and Thoresbracka not to destroy the stones and mounds under the Ulfveberg, and above all things to keep the altar at Glosshed safe and whole? In return thou shalt have a good wind to the place for which you are bound.' These things the sailor promised to do upon his return home. 'But why are you so anxious after such matters?' he asked. 'My name is Thorer Brack,' he was told, 'and my habitation is there, though I am now a fugitive. In the great mound by the Ulfveberg my whole race lies buried, and at Glosshed's altar we worshipped Thor.' Then the sailors parted from the old man, and they had a fair wind all the way to their destination."

Third spoke: "In Smaland, in the parish of Skatelof, there is a famous well. It, too, is a place where Thor's worship held on. It is said that in the place where the well stands, a young man once arranged to meet his beloved. From suspicion of his infidelity his beloved murdered him on the spot. Out of sympathy for the slain youth Thor caused the well to spring out from his blood. The folk of those parts assembled at the well every year, and played sacred games, and sang a particular song, and left offerings. So strong was the love of Thor here that it survived the coming of the Cross. After the Conversion the folk simply started calling it 'St. Thor's well' instead of the god Thor's well, but that one concession for the sake of camouflage was the only one they made. His rites were held there every year for long centuries after that time, though in the end they dwindled away."

Gangleri was curious: "What else can you tell me of the worship of Thor?"

High told him: "Besides the oak, stones are most sacred to him. Those smooth, wedge-shaped stones that are found sometimes in the Earth are called Thor-wedges, for tradition has it that they came to be scattered about the earth by Thor using them as missiles to hurl at Trolls. Aerolites, the stones that fall sometimes from the sky, are memorials to Thor. Once Thor, as he was passing through Smaland with his assistant Thialfi, met a giant. 'Whither are you bound?' challenged Thor. 'To Valhalla,' answered the giant, 'to revenge myself upon Thor, who has burnt down my barn.' The giant, evidently, had not gotten a good look at him at the time. 'It is hardly advisable for thee to measure thy strength against his,' cautioned Thor, 'for it seems to me you are not even man enough to lift this stone here.' At this the giant grew mightily wroth, and he bent to lift the stone, which was an aerolite. But he could not raise it from the earth, so strongly had Thor charmed it. Thialfi tried next, and lifted the stone as though it were a pebble. The giant landed a blow upon Thor that staggered the thunder-god to his knees, but Thor's blow crushed the giant's skull."

Gangleri, amazed, said: "It would seem that Thor is mighty indeed. It would be good to have such an ally as he."

"Yes," agreed High, "It would. For Thor in the time of heathenism was regarded as a mediator with the Alfadhir. Now, the Thorbagge beetle is sacred to Thor. It is said that because of this anyone who comes across one lying stuck on its back and arights it expiates any debt owed the gods, for Thor will intercede with the Alfadhir for them in gratitude."

Third said: "But refreshment is needed. Just go through the door on your left there and bring in the tray you find, and we shall answer further questions, for we see that you have many."

And Gangleri went through the door on the left but found no pantry or kitchen, as he had expected, but only a hall. He walked to the end of the hall in search of the location of the tray, and went through the door he found there. He found himself in a storage room, such as are near kitchens, and he heard the sounds of bustling people and smelled the scents of a kitchen coming from a nearby door. But this proved not to be what he sought either. He passed from room to room, always hearing and smelling his quarry just around the bend, but never getting there. And eventually he passed further from where he thought the kitchen might be, and passed by hallways lined with suits of armor, and halls displaying every manner of arms. He passed display cases full of cunningly jointed skeletons, and came at last to an unobtrusive door beside which stood a small table bearing a tray, upon which was a bottle labeled 'Kvasir's Blood'. Picking up the tray, Gangleri went through the door ahead of him, for he hadn't a clue as to how to retrace his steps. He found High, Just-As-High, and Third overseeing a gymnasium where martial artists and fighters of every sort were training in the arts of war. They took from him the bottle and poured it into four glasses sitting close at hand on a trunk.

Gangleri next addressed the three: "And what of Odin? How fared he at the end of the ancient heathen days? Was he a defender of gods and men, like unto Thor?"

High replied thusly: "It is in Thor's nature always to turn aside the wolf from the door. But Odin was farsighted, and could see how the struggle with the new faith would work out. And he is no wastrel, to plant seed in the autumn. So he turned his mind to longer-ranged plans."

Just-As-High added: "But before these plans were set in motion he paid a visit to the champion of the Christ, the tyrant Olaf the Lawbreaker. He was of a mind to make one last attempt to win the despot back to the ways of his ancestors, and failing that he figured he could at least have a little sport."

Third spoke up: "One evening at the king's home at Ogvaldsnes an old man arrived whose face was shadowed by his wide-brimmed hat. He named himself Gestr, and asked the king's hospitality. Olaf was suspicious of him, and reluctant to invite him in, but at last he bade Gestr enter. That night the king bade Gestr to come to his bedside, and entertain him with traveler's tales. Gestr's talk was wide-ranging, and covered even the history of the very hall they stayed in, Ogvaldsnes. Gestr spoke of Ogvaldr, an ancient king, and how he worshipped the Vanic powers, paying them cult through the person of a sacred cow. He related how that king was so loyal that he even had the cow buried beside him. He spoke of other ancient heathen kings, and their ways, and their noble accomplishments. He asked Olaf 'Which ancient king would you have been could you so choose?' The king rejoined 'I would not wish to be any heathen, whether king or any other man.' Gestr said 'It is obvious you would want to be no one other than yourself. What I am asking is this; which ancient king would you wish to be most similar to, if you had to choose one?' 'I wouldn't want to be any ancient king,' said Olaf petulantly, 'but if I had to say something on the subject then I would prefer to have the conduct and nobility of Hrolf Kraki, provided that I maintain all Christian observance and my faith.' Gestr said 'Why would you prefer to be like Hrolf Kraki who might be called a nobody compared with another king - and why would you not like to be like that king who had victory over anyone he had battle with – and who was so handsome and accomplished in skills that no one was his equal in the North – and who could give victory in fights to others as himself – and poetry surrounds him as ordinary speech does others?'"

High continued: "In this way he was offering Olaf a deal. He had described this king in such a manner that Olaf must know he spoke of Odin, and that it was Odin himself who spoke. And he pointed out to him that he had much to offer those whom he favored. But Olaf was not of a mind to accept this offer. 'Least of all would I wish to be you, evil Odin!' he cried, and threw a prayer-book at his guest. At this Odin leapt up and, giving a mad laugh, departed. But he left by way of the kitchens, and saw there the meat being cooked for the king's breakfast. He saw that it was of poor quality and, mindful of the duties a guest owes his host, even such a host as Olaf the Lawbreaker, he conjured up two sides of beef of a much better quality, and gave them to the cooks as a guesting gift. But Olaf would not touch the meat, and had it thrown away."

Just-As-High spoke: "He also paid a visit to Eric, the last heathen king of Sweden. Eric was a magician, and had prospered well from the many hidden things Odin had shown him. After Odin gave him victory at Fyriswall he had no more enemies to threaten the peace of his realm, and he turned to consideration of the future. He saw the faith of the Cross spread itself further and further in every direction, and he was very aware that he was the last heathen king in the North. So he made a sacrifice to Odin, that Odin might show him how many Christian kings after him were to sit on the throne of Sweden. Odin came to him and told him he must burst King Sverker's rock, in the heart of which he would find a tablet containing all he wished to know concerning his successors."

Then spoke High: "When the rock in question was split there was found inside a tablet of stone, set with gold plates and precious stones. One the one side was an oblong around which were thrice nine crowns, beset with the names of kings. On the other side a triangular plate with thrice seven crowns. All of these crowns were distinguished by different colors. In this way Odin answered King Eric's request."

Then Gangleri spoke up: "But what were the Alfadhir's intentions? How did he plan to get through the coming winter?"

Just-As-High answered him: "As with Thor, not everyone abandoned him at once. The rural folk; farmers and smiths, hunters and tinkers held to the old faith much longer than the city folk did. And it was a custom of farmers, from the oldest times, to bundle together the last sheaf from the harvest, especially of rye, and leave it lying in the field as a sacrifice to Odin. Some believed he used it for fodder, feeding it to his wondrous eight-legged horse Sleipner. This sacrifice ensured the field would be bountiful in the coming year. After this sheaf was cut it was traditional to drink the Wodel-beer, in honor of Odin. When the sheaf was tied it was the custom of the farmers to dance 'round it, throwing up their caps and shouting 'Wod! Wod!', which was the name by which they knew Odin. They would pour their drinks upon the stubble of the field; beer, brandy, or milk, and the women would shake the crumbs out of their baskets, leaving them also upon the field. Sometimes a fire would be lit and danced around. And this tradition continued many a long year, long past the time all other traditions had died out. Even in the years when all lands were Christian, farmers would hold to this sacrifice."

Third then said: "Indeed, Odin even had ways of ensuring

this relationship would continue. When the rye-fields of the priest named Peter Dagson had sprung up, he left them uncut. Odin rode down from the hills in giant form, so tall that he towered above the farmbuildings. He carried a spear in his hand and stood in front of the farmhouse's doorway and so intimidated its occupants that no one could go in or out. This he did every night until the rye was cut."

Gangleri asked: "Were the only folk who kept his troth in any fashion such farmers as these?"

Just-As-High said: "Not entirely. For all the years from that day to this, vitkis - those who work with the runes - have called upon his aid, and given him offerings. Him and Loki both."

High spoke: "As Wod Odin was known for centuries after, and as Hattr. These were the names by which he was called when he led the Wild Hunt, the mad ride of the dead in the skies over the earth, that takes place every winter."

Gangleri would know more: "And what was this mad Wild Hunt? Who were the hunters, and what their quarry? And how did this fit in with the Alfadhir's plans to survive the defeat of the Aesir?"

High spoke: "The quarry the Wod Hattr sought was the same everywhere he went, yet not the same. Those people who knew him best, them that met with the Wild Hunt and returned to tell of the tale, said sometimes that they hunted for one woman in particular. Usually that woman, when seen, was seen to be a huldrawoman. Other times he seemed bent on exterminating all the huldrafolk, all of the alfar, all of the landwights."

Gangleri raise his brow in surprise, and quoth: "But why? Are not they the very spirits of the land, and the habitants of trees and plants of all kinds? Why should he wish to destroy such as they?"

Just-As-High answered him: "It is because of the harvest. Thinkest thou; what is the harvest but death? Odin is lord of death and harvest both. Why, after the crops have been cut, and the land settles into the winter half of the year, it would be pure abomination to let the living spirits of the land dwell within dead husks. There would be no value in the land the next summer cycle, and no crops of any sort. That would truly be the greater disaster."

Third spoke up as well: "Fear not for the alfen-kind. Odin is the ferrymen, and his boat goes in both directions over the waters that separate this world from the next. They are brought back with the summer, when life returns to the land, and the crops are again sown."

Gangleri then spoke: "You have said that people would sometimes meet with the Wild Hunt. What stories did they have to tell of such an encounter?"

Just-As-High replied: "All who see the Hunt report the same. It is led by the Wod Hattr, a great grim form wearing a broad-brimmed hat, or else a hood. He rides a great white horse, and following him is a great train of the dead, who shout and howl with a most unearthly cacophony. Black hounds accompany them. They ride quickly indeed, so quickly that sometimes one of the hounds cannot keep up and is left behind. When this happens the hound invariably turns up on someone's doorstep and will not leave. They bring bad luck and misfortune. The only way to be rid of such a dog is to brew beer inside an eggshell. The hound will then run as fast as he can away from the house, exclaiming in human voice 'Though I be old as the mountains, never before have I beheld such a strange sight!'"

Third spoke up: "One night a drunk peasant was returning home very late. As he was walking he heard a great hue and cry from above him. It was the Wild Hunt, with the huntsman shouting at his noisy dogs high in the air above him. At this the peasant was greatly frightened, for all knew the Huntsman was very ferocious, and seldom kind, though he would spare travelers who kept to the middle of the path. A voice cried out from above 'In the middle of the path! In the middle of the path!' but the peasant was drunk, and did not heed it. Suddenly the Wod Hattr himself descended from the clouds on his great steed Sleipner."

High then joined in: "The Hattr addressed the peasant: 'How strong are you? Let us have a contest. Here is a chain. Hold onto the end of it. Who can pull the hardest?' With courage of the drunk the peasant took hold of the chain. The Hattr ascended once more into the clouds. Meanwhile, though, the peasant was wrapping his chain around the trunk of a stout oak tree. The huntsman pulled in vain. Presently he returned from out of the sky. 'You wrapped your end around the oak tree, said the Wod Hattr', dismounting. 'No,' responded the peasant, who had quickly unwrapped it while the Hattr descended, 'here it is in my hands.' 'I'll have you in the clouds then!' cried the hunter, and vaulted back onto his horse, and climbed again into the sky. The peasant again wrapped his end around the oak. Overhead the horses neighed, and the dogs howled, and the wagons creaked, and the dead shouted. And again the huntsman pulled in vain."

Just-As-High continued: "The oak tree creaked, and the peasant shook with terror, but the tree held. Descending again the Hattr spoke unto him: 'You have done well! Many men have become mine in such fashion. You are the first who has withstood me. I will reward you!' For Odin has ever appreciated cleverness as well as strength, and the very drunk are his people. The Hattr remounted into the sky and with a great 'Halloo! Halloo!' the Hunt continued on its way. Then suddenly, from above, a great stag fell at his feet. Appearing again the Wod Hattr quickly cut up the game. 'The blood is yours,' quoth he, 'and a hind quarter as well!' 'My Lord,' said the peasant, 'your servant has neither bucket nor pot!' 'Take off your boot then!' was the rejoinder. This the peasant did. The boot was filled with the blood. 'Now take the blood and the hindquarter home to your wife and child,' instructed the Huntsman. And with that he was away. At first fear lightened the peasant's burden, but soon the hind quarter and boot grew heavy. Then they grew more heavy still, until he could scarce carry them. But he feared to put them down. However, upon returning home he saw that the blood in his boot had become gold coins, and the hind quarter of venison had become a bag of silver coins. And never again did they live in want."

High spoke again: "It is most dangerous to be too close to that Hunt. Those who are not as resourceful or lucky as the peasant will be swept up by it, and must run with it until the dawn. And not all those who do run with it survive the experience. This is why curiosity about the Hunt can be a dangerous thing, as one inquisitive fellow learned. Udarser mill had a reputation for being a haunt of the huntsman's train and one night, while working late, a miller heard the Hunt passing noisily by outside. 'Halloo!' they cried. Having heard much about the deeds of this ghostly hunt he wanted to know more about them. He went out onto the mill's platform and added his voice to the cries of the hunters, 'Halloo!' Suddenly he heard a voice calling out 'If you want to hunt, you can join the Ride!' At the same time someone overhead threw a woman's leg at the feet of the miller, who, afrighted, ran inside the mill. No more did he seek out the Hunt."

Then Third said: "But it was well for the miller that he was not disrespectful. He was invited, rather than captured outright. And had he taken the Wod Hattr up on his offer, he may have been rewarded as the drunk peasant had. But there was another pair I am reminded of, one of whom foolishly sought out the Hunt. One was quite drunk, while his friend was not. They heard cries, and the barking of dogs, and the cracking of whips, high in the air. The sober man cried 'God preserve us! It is the Wild Hunt!" and prudently fled. But his drunker, foolisher friend laughed, and said 'I would fain know what the foul fiend catches! Hola, Huntsmen, give me share of your game!' Saying this he continued home. But upon his arrival there he found the hind quarter of an ox, dead many months, flung upon his doorstep. It crawled with worms and maggots, and sickened all within."

Gangleri said: "This train of the dead, these ghost riders in the sky seem quite perilous. Besides keeping to the middle of the path, and treating the hunters with respect, what must one do to conduct himself rightly, faced with such apparitions?"

High answered: "If the door to your house stands open when the Hunt passes, the Hunt will pass within and destroy everything in its passing, so it is well to close all doors when the hunt is out. On Yule eve there should be no baking, for it might attract the Hunt. On this same night no linens should be left out, or the dogs of the hunt will tear them to pieces. During the twelve days of Yule (for in those days that belong to neither old nor new years the Hunt is most active) no spinning should be done, nor any flax be left on the distaff, or the Wild Hunt will ride through it, and spoil it all. Those who break this taboo also risk being taken up by the Hunt, as foolish travelers are who are caught outside. Additionally it is well that all be as still and quiet as possible when the Hunt is abroad. Lastly, the fate of a village or household can be foretold by going out during Yule night and listening for the Hunt. If it is heard close by it will be hard, but if it is heard far off then a year of peace will ensue."

Gangleri then asked: "And is this the only way in which Odin passed those years? Leader of the dead, outlaw, stranger to the lands of men?"

High spoke again: "Yes. Once the people of a god are no more, the god passes into death. In those years Valhalla stood empty, and the gods came no more to Midgard, but Odin could still dwell in the dark places, the Outgarths. On one occasion he visited the town of Hameln as just such an out-dweller. It was in the year 1284 and the town was intolerably infested with rats. One day a stranger, most peculiarly clad, arrived in the town, and he gave himself out for a rat-catcher. He named a certain sum of money as his fee, and promised to rid the town of all its rats. The townsmen agreed to his fee readily, for rats are the carriers of plague. The stranger drew forth a pipe, and blew upon it a strange and haunting melody. In that instant the rats came hurrying out of every house, cellar, and corner in the town. They appeared in such numbers that the streets seemed to be veritable rivers of fur and tails. The stranger then proceeded to the gate that led to Lachem and Aerzen and to the river Weser. He did not stop at the bank but waded into the river. The rats, following the sound of his pipe, did likewise and drowned, every one of them."

Just-As-High said: "No sooner were the townsmen relieved of their problem when they repented of their promise to the stranger. The fee was high, and they had no desire to part with that much money. Accusing the man of being a sorcerer they refused him remuneration. At this the stranger was furious, and vowed vengeance. On the 26th of June, the day of Saint John and Saint Paul, every person in the town was at church, and the stranger again entered the town. He was clad as a huntsman, and wore a broad-brimmed hat, and his countenance was wroth. He again produced his pipe, but the tune he played upon this occasion was different than that he played upon the last. At the sound of the tune every child in the town was compelled to come out and follow the stranger. Slowly he marched them to the East gate, and the children followed him. He led them all the way to Koppelberg mountain, whereupon he and all the children vanished within. This was witnessed by a nurse-maid, who had followed the train. She said that the mountainside opened up and swallowed all of them All of them but two children, who the huntsman spared. One was blind, and could speak of the experience but had not witnessed any of it. The other was mute, and could not relate what he saw. In this fashion that rede has entered the language that says to always make sure you pay the piper."

Gangleri asked: "Have you any other tales of him?"

High replied: "In the land of Oeland, in Hogrumssocken, there are a few large stones named Odins flisor. To this day survives the tale of their origin. It is said that in that location while wandering the world, Odin was surprised by an adversary. About to fight this enemy Odin was at a loss for where to tie his horse, and in a hurry ran up to a great boulder and pierced it with his sword. Tying his horse's reins through the hole thus made, he turned his attention to his foe. But his horse was restless, and broke free, shattering the rock. This not only left the fragments named Odins flisor, but also created a bottomless bog in that spot, where the stones impacted the earth. This bog is called the Hogrumstrask, and no matter how many poles are tied together, no bottom can be found."

Gangleri said: "But still you have not told me of how Odin planned to survive the coming of the Cross."

Third said: "The faith of the Cross had won against the forces of Asgard. But Odin was clever. After all, he had died once before, when he hung himself upon the tree. Death was nothing new to him, and he used it to his advantage. In Gothland, most particularly in Smaland there was a place called Kraktorps Gard. In this place stood a barrow. This barrow was said to be Odin's, and had been called such since the conversion. For you see Odin was farsighted, and went willingly into the ground when he saw how the conflict ahead would work itself out. For what has been buried may once again rise. And being dead in no way prevented him from leading the Wild Hunt, and in this fashion he kept a toe-hold in the world. And then, many centuries after the Conversion, the farmers who lived in Smaland grew curious about the barrow, and desired to see what lay within. They had kept the old stories, and had been told it was the burial place of a god. So they went to the Kraktorps Gard and opened the barrow. When they opened it there leapt out of it a great flash of fire, that shot into the sky like a bolt of lightning. And when the farmers could see again, they found the barrow empty but for a coffin that contained some flints and a lamp."

Then Gangleri spoke: "Indeed! And what followed upon such a singular event?"

High responded: "That new expression in art, music, and composition that was called the German Romantic movement by those historians who followed it. All of a sudden the old faith of the heathens was the subject of poetry and art everywhere. Great operas were written. Poets banded together to explore this new/old mythology. And from such roots came a new tree. Some heard the voices of the old gods speaking to them again. And the old faith was born anew."

Gangleri: "Is anything else known of Odin?"

Third spoke: "He is a great lover of women. His wives and lovers are so numerous there is little peace in his home. There is a great rivalry between the chiefest of them. It is one of the reasons he wanders so! The Runemad, near to the Nyckelberg, is a place sacred to him. Sunk below the surface of the water is the ship Odin used to ferry the slain from the battle of Bravalla to Valhalla. And that he is the god of games and play of all sorts. Also that the handsomest of birds, the black heron, is called Odin's swallow."

Gangleri spoke: "So if Valhalla stood empty during those years Odin was dead, what of the einherjar? The slain who resided there with him, feasting, and drinking, and training in weapons?"

High said: "Many went back to their graves or the places where they fell in battle, there to reside as barrows wights. Over the long years on occasion someone of the living would run across one such. One time at a pastorage in Iceland a dead person had to be buried, and so the hired hands were set to the task. A spirited young serving girl employed also by the church chanced to pass by the grave when it was almost dug. Just as she was going by the grave diggers chanced to turn up a human thighbone from some ancient burial. It was of enormous size and the girl picked it up and commented: 'It would have certainly have been fun to kiss him while he was still alive!' The day passed into evening and the pastor discovered he wanted a book he had left on the altar at the church. He asked the serving girl to go and get it for him for she was fearless, and would be unbothered by the dark. She went to the church and fetched the book and turned to leave.

But she saw a man there, of enormous size, sitting in one of the pews. He addressed her, speaking in verse:

'Gone is my glowing skin-tone,
good my maid, and faded.
Look into my dead eyes, lady,
lustrous of old, though cold now.
Hacked in half my buckler
had I of yore in war; my
beard's uncleaned, but kindly
kiss me if you still wish to.'
The girl, not in the least taken aback, did so."

At this Just-As-High suggested to Gangleri that he might want to view a painting that hung in the great hall on the other side of the wing they were currently in. And he gave Gangleri directions that he could more easily navigate the maze. Once there Gangleri beheld a great painting; a golden-bristled, shining boar ran through the sky, and on his back was the image of a handsome and athletic-looking young man. In the forefront, on the ground below, were painted with striking realism a crowd of men offering up gold and gems as sacrifices to a boar that stood on the crest of a mound. In the background the same youth that bestrode the sky-boar was at work on a farm, repairing plows. There stood bolted into the wall beside the painting a little brass plaque that told that the painting was titled "Derk with the Boar", and that it was done in honor of those who kept to Frey's sacrifices in the years after the Conversion.

Returning to the gymnasium Gangleri was lost in thought, and must have made a wrong turn, for he soon found himself in an unfamiliar part of the house. It was old, and seemed disused, and looked in places to be falling apart. He saw a light around a corner and made for it. But he soon saw that the light was really around a further corner, and that he had been mistaken. But when he rounded that corner the light appeared still farther off. He continued in this fashion some little distance further, and found High, Just-As-High, and Third at work repairing an old pantry, whereing stood nothing but dust and the entrance to a root cellar beneath them. It was while picturing the earthen cavern below them that the earth shook slightly under their feet, rattling the door hanging askew on their rusted hinges. This reminded Gangleri of certain stories the old vagrant had told him.

Gangleri said: "Well, I am sure I do not need you to tell me what has become of Loki since the Conversion, for he is bound underneath the earth."

High said: "There you are wrong. For though Loki is bound underneath the earth, never to be freed until Ragnarok, still he is free and walking upon its surface as well, and in others of the Nine Worlds even. For gods are not bound to one location only. Look at the Birch Goddess, who during Yule checks on every household and its occupants, everywhere. Take Odin for example. He is Death, the conductor of souls, the Ferryman. But death is everywhere, all over the world. Such as these must be in many places simultaneously. Some gods can even be in several persons in the same place together, talking to a stranger as though they were a group."

Gangleri was affrighted: "But is this not very dangerous? Is he not the wreaker of calamity and father of lies? Is he not lord of deception? Is he not said to be the disgrace of all gods and men?"

High answered again: "It was a Christian who said he was the disgrace of all gods and men. Some gods they hated worse than others. They did away with Freya's lore nearly entirely. Loki they vilified. They twisted his stories and blackened his name, for they needed to make the heathens of those times identify their practices with the Christian ones. In such a way, thought the men of the Cross, would the heathens slowly be led away from their beliefs. And since Loki truly was the lord of deception, the father of lies, and the bringer of calamities they found it easy to represent him as a heathen sort of Satan."

Third spoke: "But the ancient heathens knew the need for these things, for they knew that the world was a hard cruel place, and that sometimes one needed to deal from the bottom of the deck. In such a fashion Loki might be called Lord of Dirty Tricks. He dwelt at the fringe of the society of the gods, as those elements of human nature that are his provenance are kept at the fringe of human behavior. Yet he was still one of them."

Just-As-High said: "That which does not bend can break. Have you ever seen a forest after a strong storm wind tore through it? Where mighty, thick oaks cracked and broke, young birch saplings still stand, for they bent before the wind. Many were the times when, for want of some item not in their possession, or for lack of some particular act not performed the gods and the world of men both would have been destroyed, or at least been made lesser, weaker things, eternally vulnerable to destruction. But such items cannot always be easily obtained, such acts cannot always honorably be taken. So Loki, Lord of Chaos, Warg and Outlaw steps in and does what no one else can do. Living outside of society he already has no honor in it, and so is free to do those things that must be done but that the inexorable inertia of custom and law forbid. Without chaos order cannot last, for it is inevitably destroyed by that same law that gave it form."

High continued: "Every action that Loki has taken, every oath-breaking, every betrayal has been done ultimately to the benefit of gods and men. Though I will remind you that I said 'ultimately to the benefit,' not 'ultimately for the benefit'. Loki's nature is divine, but it is not necessarily that he wills it so in every case. Yet such is his nature, and that of those gods around him, that this is inevitably how it works out. Remember that Thor and Loki often travel together, for not only are Loki's wily wits of benefit to thewy Thor, but Thor is one of the only powers that can keep him in check."

Just-As-High: "Think of how the walls of Asgard were built. At the beginning of time, when Valhalla was just established, the realm of the gods was open to attack by the giants. The gods all knew that they needed a great fortification to protect them. To them one day came a builder who proposed building them such fortification. He promised them he could build such strongly and cunningly that it would stand against any attacks the giants made on it, no matter how many of them there were. As payment he demanded to have Freya as his wife, and also the sun and the moon. The Aesir were loath to give in to his demands, but they struck a compromise with him. If he was unable to entirely finish his construction in the space of one winter, then he should forfeit his payment entirely. It was further stipulated that he would receive no help but from his stallion. And it was Loki who came up with these terms, telling the other gods there was no way the builder could finish in time even with a horse's help. But when summer was but three days away the builder was nearly finished with his work, such was the aid the tireless stallion gave to him. At this the gods were greatly afraid, for they stood to lose not just the mighty, wise, and wonderful Freya but also the sun and the moon from out of the sky. If that were to occur then no life would ever thrive upon Midgard. The gods started pointing fingers in their apprehension, and quickly determined that Loki's advice had gotten them into this bind, so Loki must get them out of it. They threatened to attack him if he didn't. So, ever a pragmatic deity, Loki turned himself into a mare and led the builder's magic stallion away. And when he saw that he would not finish the work in time to receive his payment the builder flew into a giant-rage, and so revealed himself as a giant. At this revelation Thor killed the builder, for giants were prohibited from setting foot in the home of the gods. Loki had gotten the other gods into trouble with his advice. To get them out of it he turned ergi, and received the stallion in such a fashion as to conceive, and give birth to that steed Odin later took as his own, Sleipner. Yet he won for the gods unassailable fortifications while ensuring they lost nothing for it. He also in this manner gained a powerful ally for Odin, a faithful steed."

Third then said: "Odin, Hoenir, and Loki one day set out to wander across the Nine Worlds. After a long wilderness trek they were hungered, and coming upon a valley of oxen they killed one, and cooked it in an earth oven. But no matter how long they left it in the oven, and no matter how hot they stoked the fire the meat just would not cook. They heard a voice from the top of an oak tree say that its owner was responsible for the intransigence of the oven. Looking up they saw it was an eagle who spoke. The eagle offered to let the oven cook if they would grant it its fill of ox. The gods agreed and the eagle dropped upon the ox an immediately tore off all the best meat. This particularly angered Loki, who was most hungry. Snatching up a pole Loki swung a mighty blow at the eagle's body. But when the pole touched the eagle's body it stuck fast to both the body and to Loki's hands, for the eagle was really a giant named Thiassi, a great magician. Thiassi flew away and dragged Loki through the worst places, banging his head on rocks and catching him in branches. Loki pled for a truce, but Thiassi would have none, but that Loki swear most solemnly to obtain for him the goddess Idunn along with her apples, by which the gods were kept eternally young. Loki so swore, and was freed to return to his companions. And upon their return to Asgard he lured Idunn with her apples out into a forest, saying she needed to compare them with certain apples he had found there. But Thiassi was waiting in eagle-form and snatched her, and flew away. Well in short time the gods missed Idunn and her apples, for they began to age and soon were grey and old. A little detective work soon led them to Loki as the chief culprit in her disappearance. They threatened to torture him to death if he did not get Idunn and her apples back. Loki agreed to go into Jotunheim in search of her, but that he would need Freya's falcon cloak to aid him. To this she agreed, and donning it he turned into a falcon, and flew off in search of Idunn. After some time he came to Jotunheim, and after some time further came to Thiassi's castle. Thiassi himself was out at sea fishing and Loki, finding Idunn unguarded, transformed her into a nut and flew back to Asgard with her. Thiassi, however, found Idunn missing and gave chase in eagle form, only to be killed by the gods upon crossing Asgard's wall."

High spoke next: "Some time later Thiassi's daughter Skadhi came to Valhalla, demanding recompense for her father's death. The gods offered her a settlement, but she would have none of it. But Loki got her to agree to accept the gods' offer if only he could make her laugh. Master of comedy that he was, and rightly judging she would find pain most funny of all, he tied the beard of a goat to his testicles, and the bleating, bellowing, running, and falling all over the place that ensued soon got her laughing in spite of herself."

Gangleri said: "But what here did Loki do that was so beneficial? He betrayed all the gods and Idunn simply to get his own hide out of a jam."

High replied: "Yes, he did seem to betray everyone. But think! If he truly intended for the gods to lose the apples of youth then he would die too! That was never a part of his plan! He fully intended to treat Thiassi as he himself had been treated, with trickery and cunning. And look what actually happened in the end; a dangerous enemy was exposed and destroyed. And a new ally, Skadhi, was won for the gods, for she dwelt as one of them after that forever. And not only that, but at no small cost to himself Loki was able to win her aid for less cost to the gods than otherwise would have been necessary!"

Gangleri asked: "So were all of his motivations here altruistic?"

Just-As-High then said: "Not at all. Loki's own skin was saved. And Loki still was able to indulge himself in a little mischief, letting the gods panic over their impending old age while he sat nearby, with solution in hand, laughing! But no real harm was done."

Third spoke up: "There is another occasion where Loki mixed his own advantage in with that of all the gods. He is a great womanizer, and it cannot be said if he or Odin himself can lay claim to bedding more women. And one day Loki seduced the goddess Sif, wife of Thor, into his bed. On finding this out the other gods cut off her hair, that all might know her as an adulterer. Now Thor was mightily wroth, and said it was his intention to break every single one of Loki's bones. But Loki swore he would get the dwarfs to make her a new head of hair, out of gold, that would grow like the real thing, so that Thor's household could save face and so that Sif might again go in public without attracting negative attention. So he went to Ivaldi's sons and got them to make the hair, and also to make a magic spear for Odin that never missed, which was later called Gungnir, and a magic ship for Frey, which could fold up so small that it could be carried in the pocket. But Loki did not stop there. He sidled up to a dwarf named Brokk, and offered him a wager; that his brother Eitri could not make treasures so great as these. The terms were Loki's head if he should lose the wager, and that all the treasures should be rendered them without cost if he won. So Eitre set to work, telling Brokk to blow upon the fire to keep it at its hottest. But Loki transformed himself into a biting fly (for he was very shape-crafty) and bedeviled Brokk. But Brokk was steadfast and only faltered towards the end of Eitre's work, no matter how the fly bedeviled him. So the dwarfs and Loki took the six treasures before the gods, that they might be judged. The hair Loki placed on Sif's head took root the instant it touched her skull, and was beautiful and luxuriant. The spear he gave to Odin and the ship to Frey. Then Brokk gave to Odin a ring which every ninth night dropped from its own substance eight new rings of equal worth and equal weight. To Frey he gave a golden boar, and told him it could run tirelessly over sea and sky and that it brought light with it wherever it went. To Thor he gave a war-hammer, and told him it would never miss what it was thrown at and that it would return to his hand no matter how far he threw it. But the handle of the hammer was rather short, for this was the item in the forge when Loki-the-fly caused Brokk's efforts to falter, and it was the item Loki pinned his hopes on for victory in the wager. But the gods decided the hammer was by far the most valuable item and declared Brokk the winner. Loki offered to pay the dwarf in gold to redeem his head, but the dwarf refused. Loki fled, telling the dwarf he'd have to catch him. But Brokk asked Thor to retrieve him, and Thor gladly agreed. The chase was short, and the dwarf was set to cut off Loki's head, but Loki told him that while the head was his the neck was not. Wroth, Brokk grabbed up an awl and sewed Loki's lips together with tough leather cord. And for some time peace and quiet reigned in Valhalla."

High said: "Here you might say Loki did much that was dishonorable, and you would be right. He seduced another's wife. He cheated at wagering. He ran out on a bet. But all the treasures he obtained are the most precious items the gods possess, outside of the apples of youth. With Gungnir Odin gives victory to chosen mortal armies. Draupnir has enriched the gods beyond what any other treasure-hoard could have. Thor's hammer, Mjollnir, has been the gods' staunchest ally. Without it Thor would not be able to stand against the vast hordes of giants and trolls. Midgard and Asgard would long ago have been overrun, and Ragnarok come. None have ever done the gods a better favor than Loki did here."

Third then said: "As strained as Loki's and Thor's relationship was, still Loki did him a good turn. When out travelling with Thor they had one evening to seek shelter in the dwelling of a poor family. The family had no means of providing them with enough food, so Thor slew the flying goats that drew his cart and cooked them. He divided the meat amongst the family, forbidding them only from breaking any of the bones. But Loki spoke to the son, Thialfi, and told him the marrow of the goats was sweet, and that Thor wouldn't really mind his cracking just one bone. So Thialfi did, that he might suck out the marrow. In the morning Thor arose and wrapped the goats' bones in their skins, passed his hammer

Mjollnir over them, and the goats sprang up again, as alive as they were. But one of the goats had a broken leg, and at this Thor grew wroth. The only way the poor family had of satisfying him was to promise that Thialfi should go with him, as his servant. And he proved to be a valuable servant to Thor, one Thor would never have gained but for Loki's trickery."

Just-As-High spoke: "And there is another thing that is important to relate of Loki's deeds. It must be said that Odin is farsighted, and has seen the end of the worlds of gods and men. And it must be said he loves that which he created out of Ymir's body, and has dedicated himself to its preservation. He saw a way to preserve something past the inevitable end of Ragnarok. So he conspired with Loki in secret, as the wise Frigga had once advised him. Then he sent disturbing dreams to his son Baldur, who was the greatest of warriors, dreams of his impending death. He told his mother Frigga of the dreams, who went to each and every thing in the Nine Worlds and obtained from it a promise that it would not harm her son Baldur. She received this promise from fire and from water, from iron, from stones, from bears, from men and women. And when this was done it became a form of entertainment amongst the Aesir to strike at Baldur with any sort of weapon they wished, for he was quite invulnerable to everything. Then Odin sent Loki to Frigga in the form of an elderly woman, who asked her what the Aesir were doing over yonder. Frigga described their sport and Loki winnowed from her, by clever conversation, the fact that she had not requested the oath from the mistletoe, for it seemed young, and soft, and harmless. Loki immediately removed himself to the woods, and plucked a sprig of mistletoe, which he was able to fashion into a usable arrow, such is his cunning in crafty things. He went to the blind warrior god Hod, who stood at the edge of the circle about Baldur. Loki implied to him that he was dishonoring Baldur by not taking his part in the sport, and offered to guide his hand. To this Hod assented, and Loki placed in his bow the mistletoe arrow. It sped true to Baldur's breast and transfixed him. At this all the gods were greatly dismayed, and Frigga most of all. She sent Hermod the Bold, son of Odin to ride to Hel and offer her ransom in exchange for Baldur's freedom, for Harbarth brought his dead son not to his own hall of slain heroes, but to Hel. And Hel agreed to release him if every thing in all the worlds, both dead and alive, agreed to weep for him. So the Aesir sent messengers over all the worlds and everywhere they went a great wailing was heard. But Loki took the form of a giantess who named herself as Thanks, and said she would rather Hel keep what she had. And so Baldur was consigned to Hel until the end of the world despite the best efforts of his mother to protect him. You see, Odin was farsighted, and a necromancer. He had summoned up a dead seeress' spirit, and learned from her the way in which the worlds of gods, and men, and alfs would end, the Fatal Destiny. He saw his own death, and Thor's, and that of the all the mightiest of the gods. And he saw a way to preserve his son Baldur beyond this dark day. For only the realm of Hel would withstand the coming holocaust. By conspiring with Loki Odin was able to arrange for Baldur's death which gave him the opportunity to bring him to the one place he would be safe, and from which he would be freed on the day of Ragnarok. Baldur would then be able to take his father's former place, and with the children of the other gods begin the world anew."

Gangleri was perplexed: "But won't Loki fight against the Aesir and all who side with them at Ragnarok?"

Third said: "This is known, from that same seeing of the seeress' ghost. And who can blame him? The other gods, angry and unable to understand what had really been done bound him under the earth and left him to eternal torture (though even while on the run from them Loki did one more thing that proved to be of great benefit to mortals and invented the net). Also his blood-brother Odin betrayed him, allowing this to happen. (After all, it would never do to lose face, as a leader, by seeming to be directly involved with such matters.) It is perhaps understandable if the first reaction the lord of Chaos has upon escaping such torture is to apply a little 'eye-for-an-eye' vengeance."

High then spoke thusly: "And here we see how Loki Laufeyarson has his honor, despite having no standing within the bounds of society. He could not have been unaware of the consequences he would face performing these deeds. But he did them anyways. Loki always pays a price himself for his actions; having his lips sewn shut, eternal disgrace, torture, eventually death. He takes risks, wagering his head in the bet with the dwarf, or even bedding Sif in the first place, that are solely (or almost solely) for the sake of the other gods. In his fashion he is brave, and honorable, and of great service to gods and humans."

Third spoke again: "Indeed, he gives many services. Though they be hard for the listener to endure hearing, his flytings carry much truth, and therefore good advice. It is well for those who hear them to listen. Even if intended to hurt, Loki is clever enough to know the truth hurts most of all."

But the day was winding down, and Gangleri grew weary. He espied an old and overgrown garden outside through a window, and declared that he should like to wander there awhile before asking them more. So he walked through the tangled plants that half covered the garden paths as the afternoon sun faded and sank into twilight. And as it departed the aspect of the garden seemed to change. It grew ethereal and strange. He kept half-hearing words spoken in soft tones behind him, and far-off giggles, but while he saw quick movements out of the corners of his eyes he never saw squarely any sources of sound. He came presently upon three men seated around a fire-pit, and it was High, Just-As-High, and Third.

Gangleri asked: "But the gods of Asgard were not the only wights worshipped by the ancients. Tell me, how fared the alfs?"

High answered him: "The alfs fared far better, on the

whole, than did the Aesir or the Vanir. Worship of the alfs, the wights of the land, the people of Holda, was much closer to the hearts of the ancients than the gods, in many ways. The Christian Saint Martin records that he went once amongst a heathen people who were willing to adopt his faith. They made no objection when he demolished a temple. But when he went to take an axe to a tree that stood nearby, the people as one rushed forward and would on no account allow the tree to be destroyed, as it was sacred to the alfs. Every village made offerings to a dwarf who lived nearby, in stone or cave. Most farms sacrificed to the alfs of the land, who were more immediately responsible for the health of the crops even than the Vanir. Many was the farmer who struck a deal with a local troll, to stay on friendly terms and keep his livestock safe. There were warriors, and other devotees of Odin who paid cult to those alfs that serve Odin as handmaids and are called valkyries. Because these personal gods were so close to their hearts, and because such matters are by nature private, and not visible to outsiders, such matters more readily escaped the notice of the Church."

Gangleri asked: "Can you tell me of how such worship survived?"

This time Just-As-High answered: "For hundreds of years after such practices were outlawed there were still to be found alf-altars scattered across the countryside. At these altars offerings were left, that the alfs might heal the sick person for whom the offering was made. Indeed, a priest of the Christian god once complained that all of his parishioners secretly attended another church dedicated to alfish worship! Also the Horgabrudar, the wise-women who were skilled in leech-craft and charm working, kept alfish practices alive. In their rituals, well into the Christian years, they would anoint with swine-fat, which was used in heathen offerings. They spoke prayers they said were mystic. Their chief tool of healing was the alf-pot, wherein they would pour molten lead when the pot contained cold water. Out of the strange swirls and shapes that resulted, they were able to see what alf had caused the sickness, and what the remedy should be. When they were paid for their services they would perform an anointing for the alfs, which would cure the sickness. This was also called 'striking down'."

High then said: "Then there is the case of Kodhran and his son Thorvaldr. Thorvaldr was a convert to the ways of the Cross, and desired that his father Kodhran accept the teachings of the bishop and likewise adopt them. Kodhran refused because he had struck a deal with an alf, who used his powers of the Second Sight to help him. 'He tells me many things beforehand that are to happen in the future,' said Kodhran, 'he guards my cattle and gives me warning of what I must do and what I ought to be aware of. And so I must have faith in him, and I have worshipped him for a long time. But you he mistrusts greatly, and also your spirits.' Their talk went on, and in the course of their conversation Kodhran mentioned that the alf lived nearby in a large and splendid stone. Thorvaldr disapproved of his father's relationship with the alf, and so did the bishop when he was told. And Kodhran would have done better to listen to his alf rather than to trust his son, for he and the bishop snuck onto Kodhran's lands at night and struck at the alf, pouring water magically blessed for the alf's destruction all over the rock that was his home. He went to Kodhran and reproached him; 'You have done ill in bringing these men here, who plot against you in that they seek to drive me away from my dwelling - for they have poured boiling water over my house, and my children suffer no little pain from the burning drops that run in through the roof; and though this does not hurt me much, it is hard indeed to hear the wail of little children as they cry out from the burning.' But Thorvaldr and the bishop continued their campaign, and Kodhran's alf was forced to leave his home for the sake of his children, and that was the end of alfish worship in that family line."

Just-As-High then spoke: "And there were some who kept

their faith with their good neighbors the alfs no matter what. During the reign of Olaf the Lawbreaker, Sigvat the Skald had occasion to be traveling abroad at night during the winter season on an errand for that king, whose name spread terror wherever it was carried. But despite this, and despite the lateness of the hour, and the cold of the season he could find no refuge at a farm he asked shelter at in the king's name. The inhabitant, answering through the door, said they held alf-blot that night, and that they were a heathen people, and that Odin would not desire his presence within."

Third said: "There were many who had a close personal relationship with some alf or other, that was mutually beneficial to both. Sometimes man or woman would take an alf as a lover or a guide. Such an alf was called a fylgja. The fylgja would warn those they protected about impending danger, and would sometimes take steps to protect them. Sometimes the fylgja would teach her mortal consort; giving him instruction in arms, or right conduct, or deep secrets."

High spoke: "There is also a spirit called a thusbet, which is the opposite of the fylgja. It becomes attached to a certain individual it takes an interest in, and follows that one around, looking ever to his ruin, and undoing, and death. Some are attended by both fylgja and thusbet. Such was the case of Gisli, who was visited by an alf who took him to a great hall. In the hall he found many who welcomed him, and saw that many fires burned within. His guide told him that the number of years in his life were as many as the number of fires in the hall. She advised him to never get involved with magic, and to never seek quarrels, and to never injure the poor or the helpless. Later he was visited by another supernatural woman, who came to him covered in blood, and washed him in it. The first alf came back to him as his bride, and showed him the hall where he should dwell with her after his death. The second alf heard this, and swore it would not be so. So just before Gisli's death she appeared to him covered in blood once more, and wrapped him in blood-stained garments, claiming him for her own."

Third added: "There is a rune-stone at Lagno, on Aspo, in Sodermanland, whereon is writ a serpentine wending of runes. Pictured there is an alf with outstretched legs, clenching in each hand a serpent. The runes tell of the alfs and trolls that a man named Slodi saw in that place. So amazed was he that he caused the stone to be raised in testimonial to them."

Just-As-High then said: "Trolls, jotuns, giants of all kinds are often enemies of gods and humankind. But their word once given is more than good, it is inviolate. While men and gods both (with the exception of Tyr) freely break oaths, trolls and giants never do. This is so well known that there is a saying in Midgard that when someone is absolutely trustworthy they are said to be 'trusty as a troll'. Jotuns and trolls of all sorts were often worshipped as spirits of certain rocks, or caves, or mountains. The very world of Midgard itself is bounded by raw elemental forces, each ruled by a particular jotun. To the north is Niflheim, a world of ice and mist, and it is ruled by Thrym, king of the frost giants. To the south is Muspellheim, a world that is all in flames. It is ruled by Surt, king of the fire giants. To the east sits a giant in eagle form, from whose flapping wings come all manner of violent and destructive storms. And the sea, which surrounds Midgard and lies chiefly to the west is ruled by Ran, the giantess, wife of Aegir. And many giants are counted amongst the gods, such as Mimir, Loki, and Skadhi."

High spoke: "There is a particular kind of alf, known even unto modern times, called the Lund-folk. The maidens of the Lund-folk are called Lund-damsels. They are the alfs that occupied and received the worship of heathens in sacred groves. Alfs are said also to live in hollow trees and also botrads, or habitation-trees. Habitation-trees are trees that grew more vigorously than other trees. Offerings for the alf or alfs of the tree were often left there. Such a tree-dwelling alf was called a Ra. Loki's mother is named Laufey, or Lofja. From her come those alfs and trolls that cause disease and all forms of sickness, and are called Lofjerskor. Dwarfs inhabit certain rocks, and they are the spirits of the land for some way around these rocks. These rocks might be distinguished by unusual size, or unusual appearance, or a hollow in the top of the rock. Offerings of blood or wine were poured into these hollows as an offering for the dwarf within. (Though if you would see the dwarf of the rock, then go to it at night, for the sun will turn many dwarfs to stone; thus they are abroad only at night.) In addition to being cunning smiths and miners, dwarfs are best known for their necromantic skills. For this reason they were sometimes sacrificed to as intermediaries with the dead. Thus offerings to the ancestors might also be left in a dwarf-hollow."

Just-As-High spoke up: "And such spirits as these also come sometimes to individuals and strike up a deal for offerings. A dwarf once approached a certain farmer and asked him to cut an ear of barley for him a day. He promised the farmer it would be well for him if he did so. The farmer went regularly every day to cut the ear himself. And every day the dwarf arrived as well, and carried the ear off on his back, panting under his burden. In the meantime the farmer's cattle grew fatter and fatter, and he hardly had to feed them at all. But on one very busy day the farmer could not get away from his labors, so he sent his man to cut the ear in his stead. But the man laughed to see the dwarf panting under such a burden and fleered at him for a weakling. This the dwarf took offense at and he returned nevermore, and from that day the farmer's cattle grew ever leaner, no matter how much he fed them."

High continued: "In the region of Harz, a place known for its many mines and underground workings, many dwarfs make their home. There dwells their king, who is named Gubich. His head is shaggy like a bear's, and his visage ancient. He keeps the sacred stone Hubichenstein, which is very tall, and all are forbidden to climb it. On those whom he looked at favorably he is wont to bestow great riches, but on those who offend him he showers troubles. He knows all the savory plants, and many came to him for healing in old days."

Third said: "There was in former times a forester, of Grund, and he had a son. The youth was bold and clever, and these are not always good traits in a youth. They caused this particular youth to be too inquisitive. He went walking in the woods one day with his friends, and their talk turned to the Hubichenstein. There was much speculation as to its height. 'That can be easily ascertained by anyone who ascends it,' said one of his friends. Immediately the youth resolved himself to ascend the sacred stone, and boasted it would be easily done. His companions sought to dissuade him, reminding him that others had broken the taboo and ascended the sacred stone. Upon their reaching the summit they were unable to get down again, and were found dashed to pieces in the morning. The youth scoffed at these stories and set out to climb the stone. When standing upon the summit he laughed, and called out that all of his friends seemed diminutive as dwarfs. The wind arose and he found it advisable to descend but alas, he could not. Nor were his friends in any position to afford him any aid. He begged them to shoot him, that he might not fall to the ground alive, but they would not. Word of the incident had meanwhile reached the youth's father, the forester, and he hurried to the spot. But once there he was as helpless as his son's friends. That evening the wind blew even fiercer, and a rain storm sprang up. So fierce was it that none could stand before it, and all were forced to retire indoors. But the old forester would not, and was inclined to stay by his son, but the other villagers dragged him back by main force. But once at home he took up his rifle, saying to himself it would only be a kindness to spare his son the fall. He returned to the Hubichenstein. On his way he noticed that it was raining only over Grund. Everywhere else there was clear skies and the moon shone brightly. On his way back he met a little man. 'Good luck to you' the little man greeted him, and inquired where he was traveling to, looking so grief-stricken. The forester told the little man of his woes, and described the errand he was presently embarked upon. But he had not finished speaking when the little man vanished before his eyes. He continued on to the stone. He raised his rifle, and his son begged him to shoot, saying that he feared not to leave the world in that moment. But before he could pull upon the trigger multitudes of dwarfs came running out of the brush. They pelted him with fir-cones and beat him with thorns and briars. They made faces at him, and yelled, and jeered, and so whelmed him that he was driven back home. At that same moment was observed dwarfs coming towards the rock from every direction. They bore iron ladders, and mining lanterns. The first up the stone was the little man the forester met along the way, and he was the Gubich. When on the summit he spoke sternly to the youth. 'Who gave thee leave to climb my stone? In strictness I ought to throw thee to the bottom, and dash thee to pieces. And never shall another so escape. But because thy father is a good and worthy man, I shall spare thee.' The other dwarfs bore the youth to the bottom, and they conducted him to the Gubich's palace under the stone. Once there the youth found the most wondrous sight. The walls glittered with galena, and the roof was a single piece of heavy spar, white as a snow-flake, from which depended crystalline lights and precious jewels of every sort. The Gubich feasted him there upon strawberries and raspberries, brought in by dwarf ladies. When the feast was over the Gubich gave him to drink from a silver chalice, and never had the youth tasted anything so exquisite. After the youth was refreshed the Gubich brought him to his treasure vault, and there showed him his great wealth. The Gubich told him his subjects had gathered it for him, and he used it to help the poor of the folk above. He told the youth that he was man's friend, but that he must be treated with respect. He desired to be left in peace, and that the Hubichenstein be known only as the Great Hubichenstein, for if ever it came to be known as the Little Hubichenstein then his kingship above ground would end, and he would rule only under the earth. He bade the youth also enjoin others to never shoot at birds perching on the sacred stone. He offered the youth as much copper as he could carry in return. These things the youth promised, and he left with his riches. But mindful of the Gubich's kindness he gave a portion of his new-found wealth to the poor."

"In sooth," said Gangleri, "the Gubich is a generous and noble dwarf-lord. Are such cordial business relationships all that the alfen-kind desire in their commerce with man?"

High said: "That is not so. Many alfs desire marriage with mortals. There was once a young knight, a-riding to the palace where his betrothed awaited him. But this knight was an avid hunter and hawker, and had spent many days riding about the forest. In the forest an alf-maid had noticed the knight in his pursuits, and come to desire him. His road to his beloved passed by an alf-mound, and it was then she saw her opportunity. As he drew near the alf-mound his ears were enraptured by the most haunting, beautiful music he had ever heard, or ever dreamed of hearing. He suddenly beheld a ring of beautiful maidens dancing together. One of them, the fairest of them, stepped forward. She was the alf-maiden who had become enamored of him, and she was none other than the King of Alf-Land's daughter. 'Come join in the merry dance with me,' she begged the knight. The knight reached out his hand and no sooner had he touched her lily-white fingers than he was whisked away to Alf-Land, which lay under the mound. There he wandered as if in a dream or a trance. He passed through great halls, and walked arm-in-arm with the alf-maid through gardens of roses and lilies of such breathtaking beauty he was inclined to weep for the joy of seeing it all. At length some remembrance of his mourning betrothed came back to him, and he was inclined to leave. The alf-lady, who desired no harm to come to him, agreed to let him go to his beloved. But upon departing the mound he was staggered to find that forty years had been and gone since he entered, though to him but a night had passed. No one knew him any longer, though the eldest there remembered a young knight who disappeared on his wedding night forty years earlier."

Gangleri asked: "And his betrothed?"

High replied: "She had long since died of grief. Even all unmeaning things between alfs and men do not usually work out without some measure of sorrow, for their ways are not the ways of men."

Third continued: "Though sometimes it works out for the best. In Smaland a well-known family claims an alf-lady as ancestor. She flew into the home of that kin on a sunbeam through a knot-hole, and was taken by the heir of that family as wife. He sired seven children on her, whereupon she vanished the way she came. The luck and renown of that family has ever been good. But on the other hand sometimes things work out very badly indeed. An alf-woman was taken with a youth out tending the flocks upon one occasion, and appeared to him. She asked him to accompany her under the ground, where she would show him marvels. But the youth was reluctant, for there was something otherworldly about the strange woman. But she pulled aside her shirt and exposed her breast, and told the youth he might suck at it. At this the youth's reservations were overcome, for he was young enough that he never had lain with a woman, and he was terribly eager. Some days later his family found him wandering, delirious and raving about the underground world he had been to, and the alf-woman. His family brought him home and forced him to eat and drink of normal human fare. This broke his delirium, but never again did he regain the use of his speech."

Just-As-High then spoke: "And betimes human folk seek out the alf-kind in marriage. In days since passed there was a hunter who was given to ranging far though the forest in search of his game. He chanced upon one occasion to stop by a lake, and saw seven swans descending to the lake-shore. Once they alighted they took off their swan-cloaks and became as human women. They were swan-maids, who in the heathen days were called valkyries. The left their cloaks on the shore and commenced to bathing and sporting in the water. While they were occupied the hunter crept up under cover of the bushes and made off with one of the cloaks. When the swan-maids were finished with their bath and ready to leave, one of them missed her cloak. The others helped her look, but none could find it. Eventually they rose into the air, saying to their earth-bound sister 'We must away, it is the dawn, you meet your fate here whatever it be.' When they had gone the hunter stepped out of concealment and told her that he had her cloak. Thus was she bound to him, and he took her as wife. But some years later, while he was gone hunting for many days, she grew bored, and idly began to look through the nooks and crannies of the house. She chanced upon her cloak, and it brought back memories to her, and she missed her freedom and the company of her sisters. Stopping only to leave her husband a letter, she departed. When he arrived home and read the letter it said that she was returned to her home East of the Sun and West of the Moon, and if ever he would see her again then that is where he must go. He had come to love her deeply, and was lost without her, so at that very moment he departed, seeking that far off land. But he knew not where it might lie, and he soon became hopelessly lost. It so chanced that he came across a strange old man in the woods, fierce and fell of demeanor. He asked the hunter what ailed him, and upon hearing the hunter's tale advised him that he knew much of the swan maidens, and told him how to find that far-off land. He then gave him a pair of shoes that would enable him to travel so swiftly he might arrive there almost immediately. The hunter thanked him heartily, and set off. He traveled over seven Bends, and seven Glens, and seven Mountain Moors, and came at last to the Land East of the Sun and West of the Moon. It lay atop Crystal Mountain, and when he had climbed the mountain the hunter beheld a great castle. Out of the gate came the swan-maid. She was most glad to behold him, for she had come to love him too, over the years. But she cautioned him that things were not so easily done here. If he would have her again for wife he must face a test. Within the castle's walls he must enter a grove, wherein horrible monsters would assail him. If he could last an hour against them, and not turn aside or utter a word of pain, they could again be together. And such was his love for her that he bore the trial without turning aside or uttering a word of pain. And they lived happily together to the end of their days."

Third spoke: "Marriage is not the only thing desired from humans by the alf, apart from sacrifices. They are sometimes known to take human children and leave one of their own in its place. It is said that sometimes the alfs' seed will not thrive, and they need fresh blood, and that when this happens they go to the humans for it. The changeling can be told by its eyes, which are far too wizened and knowledgeable for a child's. To get rid of the changeling it is necessary to brew some alcoholic drink in a hen's egg. The alf, surprised, will run off, exclaiming 'I am as old as Behmer wold, and have in my life such a brewing not seen!' The alf's kin will then rush in with the missing human child."

High spoke again: "But the reasons alfs take people inside their mounds is not always from desire for their persons. Often enough it is a matter of whim, or an impulse to mischief. Many is the unfortunate shepherd who has fallen asleep on a supposed hillside, only to discover that it was an alf-mound when he is taken inside. The alfs are not unkind, and will invite the shepherd into their revels. They will give him food, and strong drink. And if he partakes of these then he is lost, for to eat or drink of the alfs' provender is to become bound to the alfs' land, unable to leave. And if the shepherd ever does get out again, he will find that instead of a single night many have passed. Years even. There was once a wedding party at Norre-Broby near Odense. The bride left the party during the dance and went for a walk, to reflect upon the day. As she passed through a nearby field she saw that a mound there was thronged with revelers. One of them proffered her a cup and having emptied it, she joined them in a dance. Returning to her party she saw all were gone, and the streets and houses seemed strange and unfamiliar to her. She found, at length, her husband's dwelling, but no one there knew her. But upon hearing her tale one old woman exclaimed 'What then, are you the same young woman who, a hundred years ago disappeared from my grandfather's brother's wedding?' At these words the bride fell, expiring of old age."

Then Gangleri spoke: "And are people still alf-taken today?"

Just-As-High responded like so: "Yes they are, though they are taken less often into mounds now, and more often into the sky, which is where many alfs now dwell."

Gangleri asked then: "So the coming of the Cross did not affect the alf-folk?"

Third spoke: "Some it did, and some it did not. There were those who paid the Conversion no mind, except perhaps to come less frequently to Midgard, where they felt less welcome. Others sought to retain their ties to the world of humans. Such alfs as these sometimes desired baptism, and acceptance into the new faith. One night a priest was traveling from Hiorlunde to Rolskilde. He chanced to pass by a mound and was hailed from it by a small group of dwarfs. 'Whither art thou going?' they called. 'To Landemode,' he answered, for he wanted little to do with them. They then asked him whether they could be saved. He replied that he could not answer that question for them. So they pressed him to return in a year with an answer. In the meantime things went ill with the priest's coach driver. The next time he passed the mound his coach overturned and killed the fellow. The priest returned in a year's time with an answer for the dwarfs. 'No!' he exclaimed, 'you are all damned!' No sooner did he utter those words than the whole mound burst into flame. And sometimes people, chancing upon a landwight, tried to baptize the wight. Some Jutlanders once got a little troll into their power. They decided they could do no better than to make him a Christian. So they set him in a cart to bring him to church, there to have him baptized. On route the Jutlanders heard a voice from the road, though they could see no source for it. 'Where now, Gillikop?' it queried. And the troll answered 'A long way, Slangerop! I am going to a little water yonder, where I hope to become a better man!'"

High joined in: "And some alfs took the Conversion very hard. They felt sore misused by the new folk, and were of a mind to take vengeance. Once the isle of Drangey, off the coast of Iceland, was much relied on by the people living on the coast near the mainland as a source of food, for both fish and birds were plentiful there. It was a common ground for all before Grettir came to it, but after he was killed it passed to the episcopal see of Holar in Hjaltadalur. The common method for catching birds there was to be lowered by a rope over the cliffs that form all of Drangey's coastline to the birds' nests. This was a perilous enterprise, and it had its share of fatal accidents. But eventually people noticed that the most experienced were dying as often as the inexperienced, and the best equipped, those with the strongest ropes, died as often as those with the weakest ropes, and this did not seem natural. Upon examination of some of the broken ropes of the dead, they noticed the severing was clean, as if done with some sort of blade. The consesus was that the island was inhabited by alfs or trolls who felt they had as much right to the catch as the humans who came there. This went on for a long time, until Gudmundr Arason became bishop of Holar. Once he heard of the goings-on at Drangey, he determined to put a stop to it. Going there armed with water consecrated to his god he started north of Haeringshlaup and proceeded counterclockwise, consecrating the cliffs both at their top and at their base to become the property of his god. And wherever he could not reach cliff base by boat, he had himself lowered by ropes. And once he had worked most of the way around the island he found he again had to be lowered by rope. Once down he commenced saying his consecrations and benedictions. He was at this a short while only when a great, grey, hairy hand in a red sleeve emerged from the cliff wall, armed with a saber. The saber severed two of the three strands of the bishop's rope, but the third could not be cut, for it had been consecrated with the bishop's strongest magic. But they were at an impasse. The bishop could not be harmed by the saber from where he was, but neither could he rise. A voice spoke from out of the rock wall: 'Bless no more, Bishop. The wicked need a place of their own, too.' And so the Bishop promised to bless no more of the island, leaving the remaining cliff as their property. From that day those cliffs were known as Pagan Crag, and nowhere did the birds flock more thickly than there."

Just-As-High then said: "Once a man in Aagerup, in Holbek amt, in Seeland, asked his master to let him ride down to see the trolls' merrymaking, for it was the Yule season and the trolls were celebrating. He came upon the trolls' mound, and sat on his horse watching the festivities. One little troll approached him, and offered to let him join in their merrymaking. The troll gave the man a cup to drink from. But the Aagerupper saw that the cup was of gold, and on the instant turned his horse and fled with it. All the trolls in the mound pursued him. They were about to overtake him when he reached the refuge of a church, where taboo forbade the trolls entrance. He threw the cup over the walls of the churchyard, that no matter what transpired the trolls shouldn't have it. He reached his master's house just as the hands of the trolls were about to close upon him. So greatly exasperated were they that they seized great stones, and hurled them against the house, damaging it greatly. The church was soon consumed by a mysterious fire. With this sort of landwight it could be very dangerous for the people of the Cross to be abroad at the wrong times. This was especially true of Christmas Eve, which was when the trolls were abroad celebrating Yule. They raise the stones they live underneath on pillars, and dance and drink beneath them. It was most dangerous for Christian men and women to be abroad then."

Just-As-High spoke: "Yes, because of the hardships forced upon them by the events of those days, many of the alfs and trolls grew to no longer be able to even stand the sound of bells. At the erection of a church whole districts of alf-kind would suddenly clear out. A peasant walking between Mullerup and Dalby once came upon a troll seated upon a rock, who seemed to be suffering a great affliction. When queried what was wrong, the troll replied that he was leaving the district, and that none of his kind might dwell there anymore for the sheer ringing and tolling."

High spoke again: "One evening a stranger came to the Sundby ferry, in Denmark. He hired the ferry for the night, saying that they were to ferry cargo over from Vendsyssel all night, without ever knowing the nature of the cargo. That night the ferrymen observed the stranger at the appointed meeting-spot, but nothing besides him. Though the stranger moved not, the ferrymen observed that the ferry sank lower and lower in the water, as if they were taking on a heavy lading. The stranger boarded and bade them take the boat across the water. Again and again, in this fashion, did the ferry cross and recross it. And each time the stranger rode with the ferry, as if he were overseeing something, that all might go according to his desire. After the final journey the ferrymen besought the stranger to tell them the nature of their cargo. But not a clue could they get from him. Suddenly one of the ferrymen leaped up, for he had been struck by a memory. He recalled that the unseen might become visible to one who took the earth from under his right foot and put it under his cap. This he speedily did, and saw that all the hills east of Aalborg were swarming with dwarfs with small, red, peaked caps on their heads. And from that day on no dwarfs of that description were seen in Vendsyssel."

Just-As-High: "Also in Denmark, in Fladso, there was a troll who bore such a grudge against the inhabitants of Nestved that he took a great leather bag with him to the beach, there to fill it with sand. It was his intention to completely cover the houses of the town in sand. But fortunately for the people of Nestved there was a small hole in his bag, and the sand all leaked out. He did not notice the loss until the greater part of it was gone, when he was at the spot where the castle of Husvold formerly stood. He was so wroth that he threw the remainder of the contents down, where it stands to this day; a great sandhill near Nestved at the end of a long ridge of them."

Gangleri asked: "What then, did alfs never in those years get along well with those whom they had no specific deal with?"

Third spoke next: "Sometimes humans and landwights live tolerably well together, as good neighbors. There have been times when a young wife would be having a difficult birth, and some mysterious midwife none have seen before will appear and help her and baby both safely through it, only to vanish afterwards. And on occasion alfs will seek out human aid in kind, as when an alf-wife is undergoing a difficult birth."

High continued: "In the land of Germany, close to Geltorf, near Sleswig there is a hill called the Hochberg. Close upon it is another hill, the Brehochberg. These two hills were the habitations of the underground folk. For many years the country folk there were on quite friendly terms with them from beneath the hills. When there was to be a wedding in the village and pots, pans, kettles, and the like were wanted the villagers would go to the hill and knock upon the door set into the side. 'What do you want?' the underground folk would call. 'We want a kettle from you, for Hans and Trina are getting married on the morrow, and are in need of one.' 'And how big must the kettle be?' came the reply. And in this fashion the villagers could get exactly such pottery as was required. All the underground folk required in return were the leftover viands that had been cooked in the pots, which were left out before the hills."

Just-As-High had something else to add: "There was a ploughman who once observed, while about his labors, that there were broken tools laying in his fields that did not belong to him. He took them home and repaired them, and set them again in the place he found them. For this service he was rewarded with a Dragedukke, small box that held but a small amount of money, but out of which could be taken however much was desired."

Gangleri observed: "It seems that it is well then to develop good relationships with these wights."

Third answered him: "It is. But it is just as well to take care, and to understand the powers with which one deals. Alfs are not as men, and even well-intentioned assistance can go badly. There was once a poor shoe-maker, who was barely able to make ends meet. Things got so bad one day that he only had leather enough for one more pair of shoes. At evening he cut out the shoes, intending to stitch them together in the morning. When he arose he was quite astounded to discover the shoes already stitched! He examined them closely, and discovered not a stitch out of place. The hand that had stitched them was that of a master. A customer presently came in and was so taken with the shoes he paid the shoemaker quite handsomely for them. With the money he made the shoemaker was able to purchase enough leather for two more pairs of shoes. He cut them out and, as on the night before, left them out to be stitched in the morning. And in the morning he found two pairs of shoes all stitched and waiting for him. The proceeds from the sale of them enabled him to buy enough leather for four pair. That night the shoemaker cut them out and left them. But he planned to stay up and watch the night through, that he might discover the identity of his mysterious benefactor. At the stroke of midnight he observed a swarm of tiny alfs come out of every nook and cranny of his shop and set to work upon them. In no time at all there stood four pairs of shoes. The shoemaker was ecstatic, and the next day was beside himself with joy. This happened again and again, and each day the shoemaker was able to purchase more leather. He took also to leaving little gifts out for the alfs, to pay them for their efforts. The shoes sold in no time, and word of the quality of the shoemaker's work had reached the ears of a nearby duke. The same duke paid a visit to the shoemaker, and asked a pair of fine boots be ready for him upon the morrow. The shoemaker, confident of his alfs, promised they would ready. The duke promised to reward him handsomely if he were pleased with the boots. The shoemaker was so beside himself that in the evening when he cut out the shoes, for which there were now so many orders he couldn't count (for many will purchase wares where the nobility shop), that he lost track of what he was doing. He reached the end of the leather which he had that day purchased when he realized that he had not left enough for the duke's boots. That night, when the alfs came out and sewed together the shoes, he accosted them and demanded they fill the whole order, that there were a pair of boots still to be made. 'But there is no more leather,' the alfs pointed out. 'I do not care how you do it, but I must have those boots,' said the shoemaker, for he knew that alfs were magical beings, with strange powers, and he had grown greedy dreaming over the rewards that would come from the duke. That night the most horrible screams were heard coming from the shoemaker's house, and he was never seen again. But upon the table stood a pair of the finest boots anyone had ever seen, crafted of a strange pale leather. The duke, by the way, was most pleased when he found them."

"Indeed," said High, "you never know what an alf might take amiss. There was a Niss, a sort of mound-alf, that dwelt in a mound near Neumunster. A man who dwelt there once offended the Niss, because he ate his porridge without butter. In revenge the Niss played such pranks upon the man and his household and caused so much annoyance that all who dwelt there were obliged to remove to another dwelling. But even this was not enough to satisfy the Niss, for when the last person, who was carrying the broom, crossed the threshold, all there present heard a voice from the end of the broom call out 'I too am here,' for the Niss was moving with them."

Across the campfire Gangleri beheld a grove of birches,

many young and slender, those further in huge and old. Amongst the common white birches were a sprinkling of black birches, and birches with bark like silver, and birches with bark like purest gold. And he could see that at the center of the grove was a lake.

Gangleri then said: "Much you have told me of the gods, but what of the goddesses?"

High replied: "There was one most mighty goddess that nearly every tribe of heathens held in high esteem. She is the goddess of the earth, and of all things that grow, and the birch tree is her especial sign, and is dearest to her. Different names she had in different times and places. Jordh, she was called, and Nerthus, and Bertha, and Perchta, and Eartha, and Hertha, and Huldra. She is one of Odin's wives, and the mother of his son Thor, whose lightning bridges the storm and the earth. There is a rivalry between her and Odin's other women, especially Frigga, Rind, and Gunnlodh. Certain groves of trees, particularly of birch trees, are sacred to her."

Just-As-High continued: "Every Walpurgis she departs from one or another of these groves in her chariot and travels the world over. Where she goes, there do peace and plenty spring up, and the ground is made fruitful at her touch. Her folk are the huldrafolk, the alfs, and also all those spirits of living things that are as yet unborn. As you by now know, the huldrafolk live in the plants that grow out of the earth, they are Eartha's children. Walpurgis is the day she gives birth to the life of the world, the beginning of summer."

Third spoke: "But all things die, and the harvest must come at last. Summer comes to an end and all the living fruits of the earth wither and die. When this happens Odin departs from Valhalla, and meets her within her sacred grove. There the seeds of next year's growth are planted in her loins. There afterwards Odin is strangled or drowned by her, and he goes amongst the dead, as he does every winter. When this happens he leads the hosts of the dead out over the surface of the world as their drighten. This riding is called the Wild Hunt, as you already know. In this guise Odin is called the Wod Hattr, and his nature is mad and fell. But the Birch Goddess also departs from her grove again at this time, and the time of her so doing is called by men the Winternights."

Gangleri again spoke: "If she brought bounty and peace with her at the beginning of summer, what does she bring at the beginning of winter?"

High answered him: "She brings little. One of her many provinces of interest is in the household, and in those chores that are necessary to keep up a household, and also those taboos that are necessary for its prosperity. Thus when she is abroad at winter she travels the world and checks upon every household. The lazy she punishes, and also those who break taboos, as well as children who behave badly. But the industrious she rewards, as she does good children, leaving little gifts for them. She especially desires to see that all spinning be finished by the time of Yule. At this time fish and porridge should be eaten in honor of her. Also at the onset of the Winternights she goes to her other paramour or husband, Ullr, lord of winter. They travel together through the season, delighting in the wonderland of ice and snow, and the thrills of the hunt and skiing. Also she is sometimes attended by a host of the unborn souls."

Third: "But there is another reason she stays abroad during the winter months. For she is being pursued by the Wod Hattr. The quarry of the Wod Hattr is the alfar and all the kinds of huldrafolk. They are the spirits of the growing things, and when the bodies of those plants they inhabit have died, or been harvested, then the spirits that attended them, gave them life, must also be harvested, and taken in by death. For truly it would be an abomination for a living spirit to dwell in a dead and decayed husk. How could the land possibly become fertile again the next time summer came? They must be taken beneath the ground, into death. The old must be cleared away to make space for the new. But it is not just Huldra's folk who are the quarry of the Hunt. The Birch Goddess herself is, and for the same reason as her folk."

Just-As-High said: "And eventually she is caught, and torn to pieces by the Hunt. She passes into Hel for a time, and the earth rests. But Odin is the Wod Hattr, a dead thing himself. He is Vegtam, able to descend into Hel. He is Harbarth, the Ferryman, and he can call what is dead back into the world of the living. Once the earth is rested he brings her back out, back up to the world. And this is the summertime. The seed that has lain sleeping in her quickens, ready to grow. Odin goes once more amongst the living and returns to Valhalla. And the Birch Goddess forsakes Ullr and takes Odin again as husband."

High again spoke up: "Sometimes when she travels abroad her chariot becomes broken. On these occasions she might sometimes ask help of passersby, who she rewards with the chips of wood that are left over from the repair. Once she has departed her benefactors invariably discover that the chips have become pure gold."

Just-As-High spoke thusly: "Sometimes, especially during winter, trains of those devoted to her would follow her out into the countryside. There would be great shouting, and revelry, and those who followed her would speak to spirits, or even become possessed by them. It is notable that many, perhaps even most who so followed her were women. These practices continued for a long, long time after the Conversion, she was so well beloved. And furthermore those who were dissatisfied with the new faith had a way of finding this goddess, even if they were part of no long-standing tradition."

Third: "She loves children, and has been known to watch out for certain families she has grown fond of. Many ancient lines have tales, going right up to modern times, of coming downstairs in the middle of the night to find her suckling a baby or giving comfort and healing to a sick child. Such families also receive from the goddess warnings when a member of the line is immanently to die, for she shows herself to them in mourning."

High again: "Women who go down into a well, or fountain, or spring that is sacred to her become healthy and fruitful."

Gangleri spoke thusly: "Are any other tales told of her after the Conversion?"

Third answered him: "Hertha castle, on the island of Rugen, was well known as a center of worship of the Birch Goddess in heathen days. Traditions continued there after the Conversion to the extent that no Christian would go near it, for they considered it still holy to Hertha, as she was known there. Many claimed to see the goddess traveling in her chariot, accompanied by her sacred cows, to bathe in the lake in the woods near the castle. It was believed that anyone who saw her bathing was doomed to be drawn into the water and drowned, for it was of ancient times death for an unconsecrated person to so see the goddess. It was also said that one person per year was drowned in this fashion, for the goddess was taking her own sacrifices from those who had deprived her of her rightful offerings. It was taboo to use either boat or net on the lake, even by Christians. One time some reckless people dared bring a boat to the lake and leave it there overnight. When they returned in the morning it had been flung high in the branches of a tree on the shore. They knew the huldrafolk who dwelled in the lake were responsible when a girl's voice spoke to them from out of the depths of the lake: 'My brother Nickel and I did it!'"

Just-As-High added: "In the northern part of Germany a woman was once traveling up the Kyffhauser, in Thuringia, to gather wood. She came across the Birch Goddess in the guise of an old woman. Although it was but April the goddess was collecting cotton capsules. The woman was quite surprised, for such things were harvested only at the height of summer. She asked the seeming old woman what she intended to do with them, for they could hardly as yet be of any use. The goddess said only that she might take as many as she wished, and that she would soon find a use for them. The woman would not believe her, but the goddess gave her an apron-full, and a basket-full besides. The woman, amused at the foolishness of the old, departed to collect her wood. But upon opening her apron she discovered that all had become gold, and the same was true of the basket. She hurried back to the spot but goddess and capsules both had gone."

Third spoke up: "There was once a man whose wife had died, leaving him a widower and their daughter motherless. The man was lonely, and so eventually found comfort in the arms of another woman, whom he one day took to wife. Now this woman had a daughter as well, and she favored her own daughter in all things above her new husband's daughter. She had to do all of the work of the house, and her efforts were never good enough for the critical eye of her stepmother. Her stepmother grew to claim that she couldn't even stand the sight of her, and made her do all of her spinning away from the house, beside an old well. She had to work until her fingers bled and one day the shuttle was so stained with her blood that she dipped it into the well to wash the blood off of it. But her fingers were so weak and numb from ceaseless toil that she lost her grip, and the shuttle sank to the bottom of the well. She ran to tell her stepmother of the unfortunate turn of events but her stepmother said only that as she had let the shuttle fall in, she must go and fetch it out again. So the girl returned to the well, but did not know how to proceed. But knowing that she would be beaten if she returned without the shuttle she jumped into the well after it. The water was cold, and deep, and she soon lost her senses. When she returned to herself she was lying in a wonderful warm and green meadow. The sun was shining and there were beautiful flowers everywhere. She walked across the meadow and came upon a baker's oven full of bread. And she knew she must be in some fairy world, for the oven spoke to her and asked that the bread be removed before it was burned. This she did. Walking further she came to an apple tree, and the tree too spoke to her and asked her to shake it 'till the apples all fell off, for they were ripe, and she also obliged the tree's wish. Presently she came to a house, and out of the house came a great Lady. It was the Birch Goddess. The girl was frightened of her, but she spoke kindly to the girl and introduced herself. She offered to take the girl into her employ, and told her she would profit well by it, if she did her work well. To this the girl agreed, for it sounded much better than what awaited her with her stepmother. At this she was especially instructed to make the bed well, for when she shook it vigorously the feathers would fly about. Then there would be snow on the earth, as was proper during the winter half of the year. She did her job well, and performed every task to the satisfaction of her mistress, who always treated her kindly. She had meat and other good foods every day. But wonderful as her new life was, she came to miss her father more and more every day. So at length she went to the goddess and told her that much as she enjoyed her job with her, and as warmly as she felt towards her, still she must return home to be with her father. The Birch Goddess said that she was pleased the girl longed for home again, for it showed she was a good girl who loved and honored her father. She told the girl she was so impressed with her industriousness that she would personally escort her back home. She led the girl to a large door and as she went through the door gave her a sled laden with gold as a reward for her hard work. She returned to her the shuttle she had let fall as well. Once through the door the girl found herself standing outside an earthen mound, near to her home. Her father was overjoyed to see her again, and her stepmother was envious of the girl's luck and riches. Determined to procure the same for her own daughter she asked the girl how she had come by such wealth. The girl related to them all the whole of her adventure under the ground. Upon hearing it the woman sent her own daughter, who was quite lazy, to the well with a shuttle of her own. Her daughter pricked her finger upon it that it might be covered with blood and then she dropped it in the well. Next she dropped herself in. She came to the same meadow the other girl had, and set across it in the same direction. Upon coming to the oven, it asked of her the same favor. But she refused it, for she disdained getting her hands dirty. She came also to the same apple tree, and it too asked her the same favor it had of the other. But she only laughed at it and went on her way. Finally she came to the same house. There the Birch Goddess offered her the position so recently vacated by the other girl, and it was accepted. But this girl was lazy and would do little work, and furthermore was slovenly in what work she did manage to do. And she never shook out the feather bed. This the goddess put up with for only so long before giving her notice that her services were no longer needed and that she would be required to leave for home. To this the lazy girl agreed, thinking that now she would be rewarded as had the other. But when she was shown to the large door the only reward she got was a great kettle of pitch that was upended over her, and to the end of her days she was never able to scrub it off of her skin."

Gangleri asked: "Is aught else known of the goddess?"

High answered: "It is said that she often appears at noon bathing in lakes, streams, rivers, or ponds, for such things are beloved by her, and sacred to her. But when noon passes, the goddess vanishes. When the sun shines it is said that she is combing her hair, as when it snows it is said that she is making her bed."

Gangleri had another question: "What of the other goddesses?"

Just-As-High spoke: "The rites and worship of the other goddesses also did not entirely vanish with the Conversion. Frigga was and is a mighty goddess, and one tradition relating to her in particular lasted long after most of the old faith was long gone. In Lower Saxony the peasants would hold, at certain seasons, and particularly in the autumn, rites they referred to as The Giants' Dance. It was a procession followed by an old ceremonial dance, and it honored both Odin, who was the primary giant of the festival, and his wife Frigga. The ceremony culminated in a dramatic act where two swords are swung around either side of a boy's neck, and strike each other so that he is not harmed."

Third continued: "There was another well-known goddess whose reputation and rituals survived even unto the present day, though after some time the rituals were no longer performed for her sake. Ostara she is named, and she is the Eastern goddess, the goddess of the dawn. The dawn of the year is the day most sacred to her, the day when spring begins, when the day's light and dark are of equal lengths. Rabbits are sacred to her, for birth is sacred to her and rabbits are of all creatures the most fertile. For this reason as well eggs are sacred to her, and are painted festively on her holy day to honor her."

High said: "But of the lore and rites of the goddess Freya very little is anymore known. It was the custom, of those devoted to her, to write erotic poetry in honor of her. She inspired such poetry that, because her hand was in it, was so potently sexual there were few who could hear such poetry and resist passion's urgings. In heathen times there were laws that regulated the recital of such poetry, but the people of the Cross were aghast. To them such passion existed only to be ignored or conquered, and the notion of such free expression was too much for them to bear. They waged a most thorough campaign against her, and eradicated every piece of poetry that had ever been hers. They slandered her name, and even came to use it as the name of one of their demons."

Gangleri then said: "So it is well that any who love Freya seek to bring this lost art back to life?"

And High said: "Yes, it is."

And Gangleri suddenly realized that the sun was coming up, and that somehow they had talked the night away. The three offered to conduct him inside to break his fast before he departed. They took him in by a back door, that led to a long hallway lined with busts and paintings of warriors and men-at-arms.

Gangleri then spoke: "Much you have told me about the gods, and their doings at the time of the Conversion and afterwards. But were there heroes as well? Did the heathens of that age make a good ending for themselves? Were there those who were both brave and true?"

As they walked down the hall High answered him: "There is one who comes to mind first. There was a wealthy man by name of Raud the Strong, staunch in the faith of his forefathers. He was powerful and of great repute, and many were there who listened to his counsel and paid attention to his doings. He was a great chief of men, and was friend of Thorer Hjort, another chief. One day they received news that Olaf Tryggvason was sailing from the south, with a great force of men, bent on killing heathens and stealing their land. On hearing the news they gathered together a great army, and all the ships that were at their disposal. Raud had a great warship, the greatest of that style that had ever been made. It had a great gilded dragon's head on the prow. Together with Thorer Hjort he sailed for the south to meet the threat, in hopes it might be contained before spilling out over all his land. No sooner than the pair sighted their foe then battle was joined. And such a battle it was! There was a great slaughter on both sides, but soon enough things began to go badly for the heathens. Badly enough that Raud's forces were scattered, and Thorer's too. Thorer took to the land and fled, but Tryggvason landed and followed, and that was the end of Thorer."

Just-As-High continued: "But Raud was strong in his faith, and the gods looked well enough upon him that wherever he went at sea he had whatever wind he desired. He escaped from the tyrant and made it home to Godey. But Olaf followed him, for he knew that if he could take Raud out of the picture then the other landholders would be more easily bent to his will. So Olaf worked his way north, attacking all he encountered. Whole villages he forced to take baptism into his faith, for he allowed any who bent knee to his deity to live, but tortured and killed all who would keep to their own ways. When he came to Salten fjord he desired to sail up it in pursuit of Raud, but the gods had raised a storm for Raud that completely blocked progress up it. There the king waited for a whole week, but the tempest showed no sign of abating. And such was the respect the gods held for Raud that they kept this tempest up even though all about the fjord the weather was fair. Eventually the king continued on to Omd, where he conquered the heathens dwelling there, and thought to enter Salten Fjord by the north. But he found the same tempest blowing there, and his position was in no wise improved."

Third was next: "So Olaf was defeated. But he resolved to go to Bishop Sigurd, a powerful Christian sorcerer. He stood in the prow of Olaf's ship and there performed his rituals, sprinkling the boat with consecrated water and uttering prayers. He did not have the strength to halt the storm, but he was able to render the ship he stood on impervious to waves. So ordering the sails lowered, that sole ship proceeded into the fjord by rowing. And each ship in Olaf's fleet was able to follow behind it, using it as a wave break, also rowing. Thus they were able to slip by the tempest, and reach Godey. Now Raud was called "the Strong" for a reason, for none were warrior enough to stand against him. But Olaf attacked his homestead while Raud was sleeping, bursting in the door with a great force of men, and was able to have him tied up before he could awaken. And so Raud was taken. Of Raud's family and servants, Olaf had some killed, and some made prisoner, and some beaten, such as most amused him in each case. Then Olaf had Raud brought before him. He offered Raud baptism, and promised to allow him to keep his property, and offered furthermore to become his ally if he would live as a thrall to the Cross. But Raud spoke out strongly, crying that the god of the Cross was unworthy of service, and never would he follow such a one. At this the king declared that Raud should die the worst possible death, and ordered him bound to a beam of wood, with his face upturned. A wedge of wood was driven between his teeth, that his mouth might be held open. The king ordered that a poisonous serpent be placed in Raud's mouth, that he might be gnawed at and envenomed from within. But when the king's lackeys held the serpent up to his face, Raud had but to breath against it and it was unable to come near. At this the king ordered the serpent placed in a horn, and the horn placed in Raud's mouth, and a red-hot iron held against the serpent. In this manner the serpent entered Raud's gullet, and in this way Raud met his end, a free man."

Gangleri was impressed: "Truly Raud was worthy of his epithet, and of the esteem the gods held him in. Were there others like him?"

High answered him thusly: "There was an influential and renowned Asaman by name of Eyvind Kinnrifi. As with Raud, many took heed of his counsel and actions, and so Olaf Tryggvason was minded to do away with him one way or another. Knowing that if he could threaten or bribe him into accepting Christianity then most other local Asamen would fall in line as well, Olaf hatched a scheme. He ordered one Harek of Thjotta kidnapped, and made much show of threatening his life, for he was true to the Aesir. He argued with Harek about the virtues of the Cross for many a long hour, but Harek remained unswayed. Then the duplicitous Olaf put his plan into motion. Feigning mercy (a quality Olaf lacked in the manner water lacks dryness) he allowed Harek to depart, untortured but accompanied by a heavily armed escort. Once home Harek sent a message to Eyvind, who was his friend. He warned him that Olaf was planning an attack upon their land, and that Eyvind had better hurry over, for they had much to discuss, and many plans to make."

Third spoke next: "But the king's escort lay in wait on the road from Eyvind's dwelling-place to Harek's. They set upon Eyvind, thirty to one, for all feared facing Eyvind's might directly. They threw him down, and bound him, and carried him to Olaf. At first Olaf feigned reasonableness and sought to convince him to take baptism by use of argument alone, for he knew a converted Eyvind held much more value for him than Eyvind-the-martyr. But Eyvind had nothing but contempt for Olaf's arguments. Next the wily king tried bribery, offering to make him rich beyond his wildest dreams, even offering him a share of such taxes as the king collected. But Eyvind remained unbudged. So Olaf decided that if he would not bend knee then he must die, and painfully at that. So he had a bowl filled with hot coals, and placed it upon his stomach. At that Eyvind's belly burst, and he went to the halls of his ancestors."

Gangleri had another question: "Were there no victors? Or only martyrs?"

Just-As-High responded to him: "There were victors. Such a one was Hakon, a Jarl of Norway. The grandsons of Harald Fairhair had killed his father, Sigurd, by burning him to death inside his hall. They were Christians, and they set about destroying temples and god-images, murdering heathens, and levying such exorbitant taxes that the whole land groaned under the weight of their iron-shod boots. Chiefest and worst amongst them was Harald Greycloak. Their baneful and irreligious behavior so offended the landwights that nothing but bad weather and crop-failure were had. Hakon vowed vengeance, and resolved to rid the land and all its people from these tyrants. And he got revenge, for he defeated all of Fairhair's descendents, and won back for the folk the freedom to practice their own religion. During his reign he rebuilt the temples and honored the gods, and the landwights restored fertility to the soil, and the weather improved too."

High said: "But war broke out between the German Empire and one of the allies of Jarl Hakon, who had helped him win back his ancestral lands. And the Jarl was honorable, and mindful of his debts, so he went to his ally's aid. But the might of the German emperor was too great, and they were defeated. The emperor had Hakon threatened with death if he did not take baptism. But Hakon was an Odinsman, and canny. Does not Odin say in the Havamal to return lie for lie, and falseness for falseness? He pretended to take baptism for the sake of winning the trust of the nithings who so opposed him. After all, the gods knew what was truly in his heart. And once they allowed him to return home for the sake of conveying a boatload of priests to forcibly convert the rest of his people, the balance of power was shifted. The Jarl offered them all as a sacrifice to Odin, and had them put overboard, to sink or swim as they might. He then returned home to take up his resistance again. He harried the lands of his enemies, until they gathered together in a great army and strove to invade Norway. But they were thrown back, for Hakon had the backing of Odin himself, who sent his own ravens to assure the Jarl of this. Just at the moment when the battle was at its most furious, and matters were looking bad for Hakon, Odin raised such a hailstorm up, driving it into the faces of the Christians, that they were forced to flee. In such wise was Norway kept free and prosperous during the reign of Hakon, and so heathenism survived long enough to take refuge in Iceland, the one place where, on the advice of the gods, the conversion was peaceful. It was because of this preservation of lore that the old ways were able to again resurface, like a yew tree growing again from its own ruins, when the gods again awoke. It is because of Jarl Hakon that the faith lives today."

Third spoke up: "There were other fighters as well. Radbod was chief of the Frisians, who had long been on good terms with their neighbors. Because their allies were all Christians, and because they earnestly desired Radbod to take baptism, the chief agreed, for he saw no harm in honoring the gods of his friends as he honored his own. But when he stood before the baptismal font he found he had a question for the priests there standing. He desired to know where were his ancestors, and would his baptism allow them into the Christian heaven as well. The priests replied that since they were unconverted heathens they were most assuredly burning in hell. At this Radbod kicked over the font and exclaimed that he'd rather burn in hell himself than sit around in heaven if it was only to be occupied by beggars and those who couldn't tell right from wrong. From that day on he resisted the armies of the Cross and preserved the liberty of his people awhile longer."

Gangleri spoke: "Who amongst the heroes would you say was the bravest?"

High spoke: "That would be Thorleif the Wise, a seer. Olaf ordered him kidnapped, and decreed that both of his eyes should be torn out, perhaps from a perverse and sadistic sense of irony. But Thorleif bore the torture with such bravery and strength that he uttered not a sound of pain, nor did he flinch. This so terrified his tormentors that they fled after having removed only one eye."

The three fed Gangleri and quenched his thirst. As they showed him to the front door he thanked them for their tales, and their kindness in answering his questions.

"Is there any way I might keep troth with the gods and the alfs?" Gangleri asked. "And which are the days that are holy, and what observances should be carried out on them?"

High answered him: "The primary holy observances are carried out during Yule, a twelve day festival beginning around the winter solstice. The twelve days of Yule are considered intercalendary, belonging to no year. The end of them marks the new year. The first night of Yule is Mothernight, and is given to the worship of the disir. Presents are given. As the longest night of the year a vigil is kept from sunset to sunrise. During it the Yule log (or at least a Yule candle) should be kept burning. Thus the light of the sun is kept alive through the darkest part of the year. This log or candle should be saved, and next year's log or candle should be lit from it. The Wild Hunt is particularly abroad at this time, and celebrants might listen for it. If it is far away a good year is coming, if it is near there will be hardship or death. It is particularly important that all gods be pledged on this day. A hog is sacrificed to Frey, or at least a hog-shaped loaf of bread. Oaths are sworn on the bristles of the boar, in Frey's name, boasts of deeds that are to be done in the upcoming year. Places are set at table for the ancestors, and beds are made for them. The dead are welcomed, and are as much a part of the festivities as the living. In some places an old wheel is tied with straw, taken to the top of a hill or mountain, set afire, and rolled down the hill. This carries all the bad orlog of the village away with it. Divinations for the coming year are also done at this time. No spinning may be done for the twelve days. This is a matter of most serious taboo. In some places no work of any kind is done for these twelve days, to allow the earth to rest as well as the people. All who honor Jordh should observe this taboo as far as possible. In other places there are strict rules against the turning of wheels."

Just-As-High spoke next: "There are a number of different holy days that were celebrated of old in different places. The Charming of the Plough, was one such, Disa-blot another, and the Offering of Cakes the third. They would fall around the first new moon after the end of Yule, or close to the beginning of February. In some places this was a Thor holy day, and marked his struggle against the frost giants. In other places the holy day was for Goa, a daughter of Thor, another earth deity. In still other places it was the disa-blot, which was for the disir, or may also have been a remembrance for a human queen named Disa. The plough, and other farming implements were sometimes blessed at this time, to be readied for the coming planting. In some places cakes might be baked and offered to all of the gods. Today any or all of these are good reasons for ritual observance."

Third then said: "Ostara is a ritual celebrating the coming of spring, and thus also the beginning of planting. Dates this was celebrated on varied, but tended to fall around the vernal equinox. Eggs are painted with bright colors, and hidden, and hunts are conducted for them. (Eggs are a symbol of new life, and fertility. Rabbits are a symbol of this day too, for the same reason.) Other games are sometimes played with the eggs too, such as racing with them balanced on a spoon, or rolling them downhill. Eggs are ritually thrown high into the air too, and as high as the eggs fly, that is how high the crops shall grow. A procession, led by an ass, begins festivities which include a game called "Osterball". Dancing is an important part of the celebrations. Ostara bonfires are also lit. No flesh is eaten by mariners this day, to ensure safety from storms."

High again: "Midsummer is celebrated on the summer solstice, the longest day of the year. Different kinds of flowers are gathered, and tied together in bundles of nine different kinds. Sometimes these are hung in the house, to bring prosperity. Alternately, the bundle is placed underneath the pillow, and slept upon. Dreams of a future spouse will follow. A celebrant may go to a meeting of three roads and there wait for an omen or prophecy to come. Hunts are conducted for the red fern which, if found, will grant a wish. On this day the gates to the fairy lands are supposed to stand wide, and alfs freely walk the lands of humans. This is a holy day of the land-wights. Sometimes a May-pole is erected and danced around."

Just-As-High: "May Day or Walpurgis is the next great holy day. Mayflies and buttercups are gathered. If farmland is not yet turned for the planting, Walburgs are made and set up. A Walburg is a scarecrow with a spade in its hand and seems to be a representation of a land-wight. A May-pole is set up, and woven with bright ribbons. Men and women alternately take up an end of a ribbon and dance around the pole. Young women are chased by young men. If they are caught they are scourged with birch twigs, as this will make them fertile. Birch is placed everywhere as decoration, and this is a festival of the birch goddess. Her procession, described above, takes place. Dancing and revelry occurs, and games. A bonfire is lit. A May-queen and May-king are chose, and bedecked with flowers and greenery so that they are almost completely hidden by it. The Sigrblot (victory blessing) was held, asking Odin's aid in upcoming struggles. This is a very festive holy day, and play is encouraged."

Third said: "Around the period of August to September, one or more minor holy days, often dedicated to Frey, were celebrated, that centered around horse racing, horse fighting, and other horse related activities. Fairs and social gatherings were a big part of these festivals. Horses are no longer so common as once they were, but horse races are still quite common, and a day at the races would be a manner of honoring Frey."

High spoke thusly: "Harvest Home is celebrated in the autumn, at various times, whenever the harvest is taken in. For modern celebrants who are not farmers the autumnal equinox would suffice. The last of the crops, especially rye, is not taken but tied in a bundle and left in the field, for Odin or for his horse. Cries of "Wod! Wod!" accompany this, while dancing and leaping, especially around fires. For modern non-farmer heathens buying corn, wheat, etc. and leaving it in a garden or field would be a good approximation."

Just-As-High: "Winternights is celebrated at different times in different places, from the middle of October to the beginning of November. October thirty-first or November first seem most appropriate, as it is then antipodal to May Day. This is another twelve-day holy festival, and it is a period of abandon and wildness. The Wild Hunt begins its ride at this time, and the dead are released to walk the earth. In celebration of this, celebrants dress as the dead, or fairy creatures of some kind, and go from door to door, demanding treats in the form of cakes, sweets, or alcohol. If such are not produced, pranks are played in retaliation on the householder. Divinations are done at this time. This holy festival is dedicated to the ancestors, and they are invited to the festival. Remembrances are drunk to the ancestors, and as many of them are pledged, and their deeds told, as possible. Places are set for them at table. This is a time when some might spend the night sitting on the top of a grave or barrow, possibly under a hood. Either death, madness, or the second sight will result."

Third said: "These are the major holy days of the year."

Gangleri spoke: "Are these the only days that are kept holy, these old festivals?"

High replied: "In addition to these days modern folk have several new holy days. One is on January ninth, the

Remembrance for Raud the Strong. On this day the minni of Raud is given, who was killed for remaining true to the Aesir."

Just-As-High said: "February ninth also, the Remembrance for Eyvind Kinnrifi. Another heathen killed for refusing to convert, by placing hot embers in his stomach."

Third: "April ninth: Remembrance for Jarl Hakon of Norway. A staunch defender of heathendom in his realm, the western part of Norway, he chased the Christian missionaries from his realm and preserved the old practices awhile longer, ensuring they would last through the dark years following the Conversion. His minni is held this day."

High said: "That day which is called Memorial Day is celebrated as Einherjar Day. It is a celebration of those slain in battle, who have gone to Odin in Valhalla."

Just-As-High spoke: "Next is July twenty-ninth, the death of Olaf the Lawbreaker. Celebrates the death in battle of this tyrant and enemy of heathens."

Third: "Followed by September ninth, the Remembrance of Herman the Cherusci. Leader of the Cherusci tribe, he defeated a greatly superior Roman force (three legions) in the Teutonberger Forest in the year 9 CE."

High said: "October ninth is Lief Erickson Day. Remembrance for the discoverer of America (that he called Vinland), five hundred years before Columbus. This is especially important for Vinlandish heathens, as this brought ancient worship of the Norse gods onto Vinland soil."

Just-As-High then spoke: "Lastly is December ninth, the Remembrance for Egil Skallagrimsson. Remembrance for bad, mad, sad Egil; berserker, poet, man of Odin."

High finally said: "And now if you know any more questions to ask further into the dark ages between the Conversion and this present day, I do not know where you will find answers, for I have heard no one relate the history of these times any further. And may the knowledge you have gained do you good."

Next Gangleri heard great noises in every direction from him, and he looked out to one side. And when he looked around further he found he was standing out on open ground and could see no mansion. Then he went off on his way and came back to his own land. And from his account these stories passed from one person to another.

Notes

The story of Boniface and Thor is a part of Christian folklore, and while they relate the same events as I here have, they have a different interpretation of what they meant. But I have here attributed the felling of the tree to Thor, in keeping with modern Asatru tradition, as the instrument of the tree's felling was the thunderstorm, Thor's medium, and one not associated with Jehovah in any particular way.

The story of Torbjonn was taken from the writings of L.M. Landstad, and passed along as folklore amongst Asatruar.

The story of the Bohuslandish sailor was taken from the collection of Benjamin Thorpe, as was the story of Thor's well, and Thor in Smaland, and the other Thorrish information.

The story of Odin and Olaf was taken from the Heimskringla Saga, and while it is not so much a "new" story, as it is a story that relates to the events of that time and fits into the stories around it to form a larger picture.

The story of King Eric is from Thorpe, as is the story of Peter Dagson. The "last sheaf sacrifice" is drawn from Thorpe and Grimm both.

The Wild Hunt stories come from the mythologist D.

L. Ashliman, as well as both Grimm and Thorpe. The interpretation of the reasoning behind Wod's choice of quarry is my own, but I believe it to be a likely interpretation, as it is entirely consistent with available information on the Wild Hunt.

In including the Pied Piper story as one of Odin's, I am following the hypotheses of several folklorists that the story was, if not originally an Odinic story, at least from folk traditions that sprang directly from Odin's stories. Reasons for this are several. For one thing Odin is the psychopomp, and many tales are concerned with his leading the dead back upon the earth, as during the Wild Hunt. In such folktales as those concerned with the death of Bishop Hatto, the dead return to earth specifically as a plague of rats. For another thing, the Piper seems to be putting the townspeople through a test of character, and there are many stories concerned with Odin walking the earth in disguise and testing people in just such a fashion as this. The magical hold the Piper has on the children is consistent with Odin's nature as Lord of Magic. The Piper's clothing (outrageous motley, great hat) marks him as a liminal character, dwelling outside the civilized world, the place most often ascribed to Odin. And of course the ending is the biggest indication. The children are led into a mound. "Going into the mound" is an old (heathen age) euphemism for dying, for going to the afterlife.

The story of the bottomless bog is from Grimm.

The story of Odin's barrow is from Thorpe. The events following it are simply a matter of historical record, and I applied to them the interpretation that would be obvious to any Asatru.

The other Odinic details are from both Grimm and Thorpe.

The story of the kissing of the fallen slain is from Jon Arnason's Folktales, and translated and selected by May and Hallberg Hallmundsson in their collection titled *Icelandic Folk and Fairy Tales.*

Details from the Frey painting came from *The Road To Hel*, wherein it was cited that for some time after the Conversion there were still sacrifices offered to boars and from Grimm, who records various traditions of "Derk with the boar" - who makes rounds every Yule to see to the upkeep of ploughs - and hypothesizes that this was a survival of Frey-lore.

The stories of Loki are all ancient, and well known from other Eddic sources. But as was mentioned in the body of this work, it seems most likely that the extremely demonic, evil nature Loki is painted with is likely in some part due to political issues from the Christian church seeking to convert heathens. This seems to be indicated by such matters as the rather inconsistent details this view of Loki as a "Norse Satan" creates, such as the fact that Loki's own death from old age would have resulted had his intention really been to deprive the gods of Idunn's apples. As more than enough damage seems to have been done to his character in this way already, and as at least in parts of the modern Asatru community the stories of Loki have been reinterpreted in a more balanced, integrated manner, I decided to re-present them this way as well.

The alf stories were taken variously from Grimm, Thorpe, Ashliman, *The Road To Hel*, *Nordic Religions in the Viking Age*, and *A Piece of Horse Liver*. The story of the consecration of Drangey came from Arnason. Specifically that the Jotuns were worshipped as gods, and not merely seen as the foes of gods, I have accepted from *Horse Liver*, and the details of late survivals or alfish churches from Thorpe. The story of the shoemaker and the elves is a classic fairy tale, and I here presented it with an older ending that I heard in childhood, because I thought it better reflected an aspect of ancient heathens' views of alfs that is more suppressed in modern times.

That Jordh, Nerthus, Bertha, Perchta, and Huldra are the same goddess is not recorded anywhere in ancient sources. Nevertheless Grimm definitively states that the names are etymologically related, and in his view they were all the same goddess, with different forms of the same name attributed to her in different times and places (like Odin is variously Woden, Wuotan, Odhinn, Odin). Furthermore the many shared details of these goddess' stories are too numerous to be ignored. For one thing Nerthus, Bertha, Perchta, and Huldra all have yearly processions, specifically in a chariot, that are supposed to spread fertility and good luck everywhere. Stories of these goddesses all have the common element of the chariot breaking and the goddess being helped by a poor man who receives the broken wood-chips as a reward, which later turn into gold. Nerthus' sacrifice is to have the slaves and/or priests involved in the procession ritual to be drowned. Huldra receives sacrifices by drowning as well. These goddesses all have lakes, ponds, and wells as holy places. Bertha and Perchta specifically are birch goddesses; birch is the tree sacred to them. The birch was also traditionally the symbol of spring, fertility, and the earth to the ancient Norse. Nerthus not only is goddess of the earth (as Jordh is), but she resided in a grove of sacred trees, and while it is not recorded which tree specifically, the most common sacred trees to the ancient Norse were the birch, the yew, and the oak. The yew is most associated with Odin, the oak with Thor, and elsewhere the birch with goddesses. Bertha, Perchta, and Huldra also share in common yearly rounds to check up on the spinning work of mortal women. The identification I made with the birch goddess as the quarry of the Wild Hunt is guesswork, but educated guesswork. The quarry in modern folklore survivals is an alf or a huldrawoman, and these are the folk of the birch goddess (most explicitly seen with Huldra). Some of these stories give the quarry as every huldrawoman, but some give it as one particular one. Asking "why does Nerthus make a *second* procession at the time of Winternights", I thought of the nature of the Wod Hattr's quarry, and this seemed an interpretation consistent with Indo-European traditions. That the birch goddess takes Ullr as consort during the winter half of the year comes from combining that very legend which is specific of Huldra with the fact that Saxo says that when Odin is away wandering, Ullr takes his place ruling. While to some this all might seem too far out on a limb, I believe that because goddess lore is lacking in what survives to us of primary sources, we need to do whatever reconstruction work we reasonably can, and I think the evidence shows that this is a *reasonable*, if not exact, rendition of the birch goddess' ancient lore.

The specific tales of the birch goddess come from Grimm, Thorpe, and Ashliman.

The Frigga lore comes from both Thorpe and Grimm.

The Ostara information is from both Bede and Thorpe.

The hero stories are from the Sagas, and are thus not really new, but as they relate specifically to the time of the Conversion they seemed in keeping with the theme here. Also, they are nowhere collected all in one place, and so it seemed appropriate that they should be.

The holy day rites are from Thorpe, Grimm, and *The Road To Hel.*

Resources

Adhalsteinsson, Jon Hnefill. *A Piece of Horse Liver: Myth, Ritual and Folklore in Old Icelandic Sources.* Translated by Terry Gunnell and Joan Turville-Petre. Reykjavik: University of Iceland, 1998.

Davidson, H.R. Ellis. *The Road to Hel: A Study of the Conception of the Dead in Old Norse Literature.* New York: Greenwood Press, 1968.

DuBois, Thomas A. *Nordic Religions in the Viking Age.* Philadelphia: University of Pennsylvania Press, 1999.

Hallmundsson, May and Hallberg, eds. *Icelandic Folk and Fairy Tales.* Reykjavik: Iceland Review, 2002.

The Poetic Edda. Translated by Lee M. Hollander. Austin: University of Texas Press, 1994.

Sturluson, Snorri. *Edda.* Translated by Anthony Faulkes. London: Everyman, 1997.

Thorpe, Benjamin. *Northern Mythology: From Pagan Faith to*

Local Legends. Hertfordshire, England: Wordsworth Editions, 2001.

Other works consulted include:

The writings of the Venerable Bede

Selections from the four-volume *Teutonic Mythology* by Grimm

The work of L.M. Lanstad

Heimskringla Saga

Folklore and Mythology Electronic Texts, an internet collection of texts edited and/or translated by D.L. Ashliman: http://www.pitt.edu/~dash/folktexts.html